BOB LORENTSON

HOLD THE APOCALYPSE PASS ME A SCIENTIST PLEASE

and
Other Humorous Essays
from an Optimist
in Dreamland

Publisher, Copyright, and Additional Information

Hold the Apocalypse, Pass Me a Scientist Please by Bob Lorentson

Copyright © 2021 by Bob Lorentson
All rights reserved. No part of this book may be reproduced or transmitted in any form or by any means, electronic or mechanical, including photocopying, recording, or by any information storage and retrieval system without the written permission of the author, except where permitted by law.
For permissions contact: bob.lorentson@gmail.com

ISBN- 9798454735616

Cover design and interior design by Rafael Andres

Praise for *Hold the Apocalypse*
Pass Me a Scientist Please

So good I completely lost track of time while reading this. Is it still 1991? (Lucy T., Serenity Home)

This pre-apocalyptic book is not nearly as depressing as all those post-apocalyptic books that have been flooding the market lately. (C. McCarthy)

This book was the perfect size to balance a warped table leg. (Rick M. – 'This Old Barn')

Astonishing! There were words, sentences, and even whole paragraphs in this book that jumped off the page. I wish I could find them again. (Tim O. – author of *Dude, Where's My Shrooms?*)

Finally – A book worth its weight in cubic zirconia! (Honest Don – The Pawn King)

This would be a heck of a book if it had bleeping illustrations. (Jeff B. - A (not so) graphic artist)

Not as funny as *The Stinky Cheese Man*. (Carl, Grade 6)

If I say I like this book will people find out who I am? Do you offer reviewer protection? (The Masked Writer)

This book is either a desperate cry for help, or for more real scientists. (Homer S. - A real scientist. Really.)

I wish I had read the essay about animal arsonists BEFORE my dog burned down my house. (Homeless in Oklahoma)

*For Rosemarie, whose smile and laugh
I couldn't live without. (Not to mention the crazy voices,
funny names, and silly songs.)*

Bob Lorentson is a retired environmental scientist and an active daydreamer. When not writing or dreaming, he hikes, bikes, kayaks, plays guitar, travels, reads, gardens, drinks beer, and wonders if the Baltimore Orioles will ever be a serious baseball team again. He lives in East Haddam, CT with his wife and two rescue animals.

Table of Contents

The Complete History of Mankind _____ 6

Coyotes - Get Used to Them _____ 10

Brain Wars - The Gender Variations _____ 13

Animal Arsonists _____ 17

What Do We Have to Lose? _____ 21

Contemplate This _____ 24

Don't Believe It _____ 25

Do Birds Think? _____ 26

Take Your Mind for a Walk _____ 30

The Dirt on Forest Bathing _____ 34

Parenting, A Terrifying Voyage into the Unknown _____ 37

Dancing to Your Circadian Rhythm _____ 39

It's Your Fault _____ 42

Divided We Stand _____ 43

Things _____ 44

The Age of Dogs _____ 45

Boredom – It's Not Just for the Boring _____ 48

Watch Out for Night Watchmen _____ 52

World Migratory Bird Daze _____ 54

The Pursuit of Happiness Can Leave You Exhausted _____ 57

Who's Winning? _____ 60

Bonsai – The Abhorrent, yet Artful, War on Trees _____ 61

DIY Brain Zapping _____ 63

In Your Face	66
Good Company for Endangered Animals	68
Ceilings are not Limitations	72
Isaac Newton	75
Robert Oppenheimer	76
Sigmund Freud	77
Philo T. Farnsworth	78
Floors - It Doesn't Get Any Lower	79
The Great Viking Makeover	81
How Smart are Squirrels?	84
Cloudy With a Chance of Daydreams	88
Brain Power	91
The Path	93
Don't Wait Up	94
Cat Research for Dummies	95
Hope on the Ropes	99
Classical Anatomy - Bach vs Beethoven	101
Collecting – A Hobby for Psychoanalysts	104
The Connecticut State Animal You've Never Seen	107
Seashells	110
The Big Trick	111
The Trouble With Amoebas	112
Selfish to the End	113
Food Fight at the Bird Feeder	115
Fishbowl Fantasies	118
Brain Farts - The Blame Game	121

Title	Page
Are You Looking at Me?	125
What's the Hurry?	128
If Keeping the Faith, Turn Down the Temperature	130
FermentingTrouble - Animals and Alcohol	133
Walk This Way	137
Long Live the Sun	141
Calling God	144
Room for One	146
Who's Smarter?	147
Think Those Pounds Away	148
Bats – Be a Friend, not Afraid	151
Golf – The Thrill is Gone	154
Our Minds - Whose Side are They On?	157
Destiny – The Legend	161
Galileo Galilei	163
The Traffic	164
Tryst at the Trust	166
The Butterfly - What's in a Name	167
The Difference between Frogs, Herons, and Novelists	171
Are the Trees Being Silenced?	174
Dolphins vs. Sharks	177
The Doomsday Dance	181
Bibliography	184

FOREWORD: HOLD THE APOCALYPSE PASS ME A SCIENTIST PLEASE

If the title to my collection of essays fooled you into purchasing this book because you were looking perhaps for a little hope against the approaching apocalypse and collapse of civilization, I'm sorry. There is no hope. And what chance did civilization ever have anyway against the existential threats of reality TV, virtual reality games, and a real reality that makes them both look like the winners in a 'Save the Earth' contest.

Add in the mounting evidence that neanderthal DNA is more widespread in our population than we had believed, and that Homo sapiens, at least the Wise Man aspect that the name suggests, is less prevalent than we had believed, and we can see why the Doomsday Clock has moved closer to midnight than even Cinderella got. (See "The Complete History of Mankind.") And her coach still turned into a pumpkin. From where I sit, turning into something from the vegetable kingdom would be a big improvement over what we're likely to turn into.

Please don't let the threat of an imminent apocalypse scare you from reading on however. What would you do instead? Clean the house? Pay the bills? Prune the shrubs? If the End of Days is truly peeking at us from around the corner, it might just be a better use of our time to sit back and review all the fun times we've had; the human, animal, and other (trees, clouds, God, etc.) behaviors that made us laugh as we questioned our existence. My essays can help with this. Who knew that those questions were all moot and that we'd soon be questioning our demise instead? My essays won't be much help with this I'm afraid.

With these essays, my humble aim is to help you enjoy your last years on earth without the acrimony and finger-pointing that is bound to happen when we go extinct. Instead, how about learning how to understand your cat with "Cat Research for Dummies," or how to lose weight by merely using your brain with, "Think Those Pounds Away." If your brain is not quite up to these tasks, please don't despair. "Take Your Mind for a Walk," and "DIY Brain Zapping," can show you how to improve it. If you find that your brain is still not up to it, you can always read about the intelligence of some of the animals that are likely to enjoy earth a whole lot more after we're gone, with "Do Birds Think?" and "How Smart are Squirrels?" And if these types of offerings still make you yawn and reach for the TV remote, well, there's always "Boredom – It's Not Just for the Boring."

The thing is, it does no one any good to sit around whining about the mess that we've gotten ourselves into. So it didn't turn out as expected. We didn't end war, hunger, disease, or country music. We never got to enjoy the satisfaction of that perfect beer, despite the herculean efforts of 8,257 craft breweries in the U.S. alone. Some things just weren't in the stars, including us. I know so many of us had figured that at some point before the final countdown, we'd at least have had the thrill of blasting off into space in search of a new sun and planetary combination to call home.

I hate to say get over it, because I know that good-byes can be hard, especially to a planet that didn't do anything to deserve us, that was always there for us through thick (heads) and thin (skin). The scientists have repeatedly tried to wake us up to the fact that the Doomsday Clock is ticking. Loudly. But not even these Superheroes have an alarm THAT powerful, not when our own untrustworthy brains are telling us the bedtime stories we want to hear. Who wants to hear "Goodbye Earth" when you can hear "Goodnight Moon" for the thousandth time, and go back to sleep knowing that the big, bad scientists haven't yet figured out how to penetrate our dreams. (See "Our Minds – Whose Side are They On?" and "The Doomsday Dance.")

It's enough to make anyone think that the Pursuit of Happiness is like a dog chasing a car. If we could somehow avoid getting run over and actually catch it, would we even know what to do with it? (See "The Pursuit of Happiness Can Leave You Exhausted.")

Our loss will be the dolphins gain, as the species with the next biggest brains. I hope they have better luck using them than we did. A word of advice to any dolphins reading this: Stay in your schools. You'll need to know more than tail-walking and ring fetching to succeed in this fish eat fish world. Especially being an entitled mammal in a fish suit. Simply being the class of the oceans won't be enough. (See "Dolphins vs. Sharks.")

Let's face it, we've all had plenty of opportunities to practice saying good-bye, whether we've taken advantage of them or not. Since the 16th century alone, humans have driven at least 680 vertebrate species to extinction, so it's not like we can claim ignorance or anything. Then again, humans never really have to CLAIM ignorance, it just seems to always be there, like face mites, or those hidden faces we all see staring at us from inanimate objects. (See "In Your Face," and "Are You Looking at Me?")

Don't worry, my essays on these and other unusual subjects don't run from the ignorance. Not even "Brain Farts – the Blame Game." They embrace it, shine a light on it, and turn it upside down and inside out. It's not my fault if any of the stuff survived. But you readers can help. And have some fun while you're at it. See how much ignorance you can find. Think of it as 'Where's Waldo' for adults.

But seriously, speaking of faces, please put on a brave one for any animals that might survive us. They have given us so much. The cats, dogs, birds, fish, giant Malabar purple squirrels, and others in these essays all had a big part to play in making our lives fuller, funnier, and more fantastic, at least when they weren't intoxicated, or busy setting fires to get back at us. (See "Fermenting Trouble – Animals and Alcohol," and "Animal Arsonists.") I do sincerely want to wish the best of luck to any of them left alive after we're gone. Especially the kangaroos. I've always had a soft spot for the kangaroos.

A final note: Well, I guess that didn't come out as optimistic as I thought it would. In retrospect, stating at the outset that there is no hope probably set the wrong tone for this book. But what's done is done. I swear it gets better. Most of the essays in this book have nothing whatsoever to do with apocalypses, of any sort, the only subject where I tend to let a little negativity creep in. OK, a lot of negativity. But I have gotten quite attached to this world, and I just hate to think about leaving it to the sharks and cockroaches. They really won't do much for the market value of the place either.

Most of the time I swear I'm an optimist, and for that, I have to thank the scientists. In writing these essays, I have consulted them often, in part to get the facts straight, but also because I appreciate their no-nonsense approach to examining everything from tree communication to, well, nonsense. (See "Are the Trees Being Silenced?" and "Golf – The Thrill is Gone.") They are a courageous lot, these scientists, who consistently go to bat for earth and all its inhabitants. They'll even go to the farthest reaches of the universe, perhaps to let us know they're not biased. Of course, they really could be secretly searching for that new inhabitable planet they can decamp to, but I somehow don't think they'd leave us holding the bag like that. I'm pretty sure they'd at least give us the chance to leave our baggage behind. It would be a hard decision, I know, because we do have rather a lot of it.

Which is why I say: Hold the Apocalypse - Pass Me a Scientist Please.

THE COMPLETE HISTORY OF MANKIND

When the first early humans debuted on the world stage 2 -3 million years ago in Africa, all they would have had for an audience is a bunch of almost human Australopithecus types and some other dead-enders, not exactly the kind you'd want to bring home to mother. Unless your mother was more of a smaller-brained, knuckle-dragging Australopithecus type herself who hadn't yet fully committed to terrestrial living. Having an almost human mother would have been hard to live down, even in those times, and is likely the reason some of the new early humans started to think about moving out of Africa.

Those early humans were no prize themselves, consisting at various times and places of the likes of Homo habilis, Homo erectus, Homo heidelbergensis, and Homo neanderthalensis, among other species who never really got it. Take H. habilis for instance, whose name means 'handy man'. He was known for being 3 ½ feet tall and for using stone tools, so how handy could he have been? What with his smallish brain, he could not appreciate the finer things in life, never progressing beyond the 'eat or be eaten' stage of thinking. That should have been a no-brainer, but as he was also known for going extinct some 1.5 million years ago, he obviously didn't see the future in brains.

Before he left though, H. habilis may have been considerate enough to pass along some of his genes to H. erectus, whose name means 'erect man'. For a time this was an apt name, as H. erectus measured 5 – 6 feet tall when he was introduced 2 million years ago. When he went extinct 110,000 thousand years ago however, he wasn't erect, and could only be measured horizontally. It was too late to change his name by then. H. erectus had a still bigger brain and developed weapons, and so progressed from a 'eat or be eaten' to a 'kill or be killed' philosophy. His enemies just shrugged and killed him anyway.

H. erectus was the first early human to discover Europe and Asia. There was plenty of elbow room in those places then, which, oddly enough, he may not have actually needed, as the fossil record so far indicates that he may not have had any elbows. He had feet, and that's all that mattered to him. That, and the female of the species. Females of other species may have occasionally mattered to him too, if we're to be honest about it.

H. heidelbergensis was the Heidelberg Man, and he didn't care who knew it because his brain had grown to 1.9% of his body weight since ditching H. erectus. He knew it and that was enough, despite those who called him an intermediate species behind his back. He was 5 ½ feet tall, controlled fire, hunted in groups, and hated to be reminded that he only lived in the Mid-Pleistocene, believing himself more advanced than he was. H. heidelbergensis made his home both in Africa and Europe, and you know how that goes. Pretty soon, or about 300,000 years ago, the families stopped communicating, the European side changed their names to H. neanderthalensis, the African side to H. sapiens, and they all went along pretending the other didn't exist.

H. sapiens remained busy throughout Africa and the Middle East, then at the beginning of their Grand World Tour they thought they'd be the bigger species and went first to Europe to pay a visit. They were shocked by what they found. H. neanderthalensis had simply become Neanderthals, with limited speech capabilities, a receding forehead, and a double-arched brow ridge to go with a stocky, short-limbed body. The Neanderthals may have been apex predators and cooked their food, with a larger brain even than H. sapiens, but as evidenced by their low reproductive rate, it didn't even impress the women. It certainly didn't impress H. sapiens, and before long they were fighting like relatives everywhere. DNA testing indicates they did kiss and make up on occasion.

Homo sapiens, as we all know, is the Wise Man, and he knew that stone tools were so Middle Paleolithic. He also knew that he couldn't let the Neanderthals drag him down while transitioning to the Upper Paleolithic around 40,000 years ago. So he did what he had to and demonstrated what a big brain is really good for as he helped the Neanderthals on their journey to extinction. What can you say, he had that kind of talent. Still does to this day.

At some point around then H. sapiens became alternately known as the Early Modern Humans, or Cro-Magnon Men, because they all lived in a cave in

France. They were also known for telling stories around the fire, singing, and drawing pictures on the cave walls of the other creatures they were helping on their journeys to extinction, like the wooly mammoth, the wooly rhinoceros, and other wooly animals. They were not wooly themselves, and were not about to let some new Ice Age turn them into sheep.

Anyway, time passed as it usually does, and the Early Modern Humans became the Modern Humans, who are known for inventing things like pollution, over-population, pandemics, a new type of global warming, nuclear weapons, and conspiracy theories. Interestingly enough, at this very moment the Modern Humans are on the cusp of becoming the Late Modern Humans.

COYOTES GET USED TO THEM

The coyote is largely a solitary, nocturnal creature. Because it has nothing better to do, it goes around marking its territory with urine. I suppose that explains pretty well why it's solitary and nocturnal. Its pelt is so undesirable that it is worth more to it than to a hunter. The coyote is also susceptible to more diseases than any other carnivore in North America. One could easily conclude from all this what even Mother Nature thinks of the coyote.

And in case that's not enough to put you off, coyotes do not make good pets. For one thing, their breath is terrible, likely because of their diet, which includes skunks, porcupines, cats, dogs, week-old carcasses, roadside trash, egg salad sandwiches, and the odd human. Odd humans would include sleepwalkers, owners who forget to feed them, and people who spray themselves with deer scent before prowling the woods at night.

Coyotes will also, more often than not, wake you up from a sound sleep by howling for no good reason. At least if they have a reason, they've never shared it. It could be just because they know it gets under our skin and gives us the heebie-jeebies, and is that the kind of animal you'd want in your house? Aren't children and relatives enough?

Another thing about coyotes is that you can't trust them. They don't walk so much as slink, which practically announces their guilt about something. The only other creatures that slink are weasels and cat burglars, and you know you can never leave your best silver out with them around. Or your cat. And believe it or not, coyotes can tiptoe. Ask yourself why they would do this if they weren't up to something. The old Navaho had a saying: Trust a coyote once, shame on me. Trust a coyote twice, don't ever make a deal with a white man.

The very idea that coyotes might make good pets probably comes from two things. The first of course is that they look like dogs. In fact their scientific name, canis latrans, means "barking dog". Don't let that fool you. The Aztecs tried naming them too – it's where the name coyote originated. They also tried taming them. Just ask yourself when the last time was you remember seeing an Aztec. Just saying.

The other thing is that coyotes have become largely habituated to humans, and have even been mating with our dogs, trying for some reason to get still closer to us no doubt. As large predators like wolves became eliminated from areas, coyotes moved in to pick up the pieces. I guess somebody had to before we were up to our ears in skunks and animal carcasses. But they have become so adaptable that they now appear comfortable with us to the point that they can be found pretty much everywhere these days except for the lingerie section of department stores.

All this is to say that while coyotes have accepted us, it doesn't seem like the reverse will be coming true any time soon. Even their conservation status is noted as "least concern," although I don't believe this to be entirely accurate. For years, the U.S. Government has periodically engaged in all out campaigns to reduce their populations, spending over $30 million and killing at least a half million of them. From each however, the coyote has emerged more numerous than before. I believe this has caused quite a lot of concern.

No less a figure than Mark Twain even weighed in, when he said of a coyote, "It is so spiritless and cowardly that even while his exposed teeth are pretending a threat, the rest of his face is apologizing for it." In my opinion, coyotes have something in common with Mr. Twain. You can never take either of them seriously. It might be what kept Twain back as a writer. It might also be what keeps coyotes from being respectable animals.

BRAIN WARS
THE GENDER VARIATIONS

By now, most of us have likely noticed that there are significant differences in the way the brains of men and women work. Or don't work, as the case may be. Neuroscientists explain these differences with highly technical scientific jargon about places in the brain like Broca's area and Wernicke's area, all of which makes the brain seem more like Area 51 to me. It should be noted however that these explanations can differ substantially among neuroscientists. This should not be surprising, as neuroscientists also come in different genders. But as few of us can understand neuroscientists of any gender, I've taken it upon myself to try and act the part of interpreter.

- Let's get this out of the way straight off. Men have larger brains than women. This is no doubt because men are always subjecting their brains to strenuous workouts. Women question whether drinking beer while solving the world's problems with friends can be called workouts, but then women question everything men do. If they had larger brains they

might seek answers instead of merely asking questions.
- Women have more brain cells than men, which seems a suspicious way around the size discrepancy. The neuroscientists seem to be silent on the reasons for this, but women tell me it's likely how they can avoid doing stupid men things. And then they go on and on listing those things. I think I heard the words war and football, and something about not listening to them, though I can't swear to it. Regardless, it seems one thing is clear anyway – they have men to thank for those extra brain cells. I won't hold my breath waiting for a thank you.
- Men and women use different parts of their brains while thinking. This gets fairly complicated, but in common language these are known as either the right parts or the wrong parts. To make it even more confusing, sometimes the right parts are wrong, and vice versa.
- Male and female brain neurons take up significantly different amounts of dopamine, which is a brain chemical that acts as a mood enhancer. This may be because men's neurons can only be activated by an on-off switch, while women's neurons are believed to be activated by a randomly operated dimmer-type switch with thousands of gradations. Women love to flaunt this feature over men, who can only respond by turning their neurons on or off, or by bragging about their larger brains.
- Women experience more brain pain from pressure than men. Men don't feel much brain pain from pressure, unless it's coming from women. Women

experience more brain pain in general, and list coexisting with men as the primary reason. Men list bragging about their larger brains as the primary reason for coexisting with women.

- Women have greater language skills than men and so are more communicative. This is because of their larger temporal and frontal lobes. Women like to remind men that it is these complex language skills that separate humans from other animals, including most men. Men generally respond by either grunting angrily, grabbing another beer, or turning up the volume on the football game. Some even do all three.
- Men tend to be better at math, thanks to their larger parietal lobes. Unfortunately, this lobe is not the lobe it used to be, having been rendered largely obsolete by electronic technology. To rub it in, women are better at multi-tasking, as any male can confirm by watching them easily juggle electronics like computers, calculators, phones, and guided robotic surgical tools, all while criticizing them.
- Women handle stress better than men, all thanks to the release of a hormone called oxytocin. Men release oxytocin too, though for them it is immediately pummeled into submission by the male hormone testosterone, whose job it is to patrol the brain and root out all weak, pacifist leaning hormones. Thanks to testosterone, men have long known that stress is better handled with beer than oxytocin anyway.
- Women have better long-term memory, and a better memory of faces. This is possibly because the

part of the brain associated with blame is more highly developed in women. Men have better short-term memory, and a better memory of things. This is possibly because the part of the brain associated with beer is more highly developed in men.
- Perhaps most importantly, extensive IQ testing has revealed that neither gender is more intelligent. The testing however does show differences. Women's IQs tend to be bunched around the average, while men's are more likely to fall into either high or low extremes. Which extreme likely depends on the quantity and quality of either the women or beer in their lives.

ANIMAL ARSONISTS

Who among us hasn't always believed that homo sapiens is the only species with the ability to control fire? We've practically lorded that talent over the other animals from the beginning, using it for everything from campfires to keep us safe from saber-toothed tigers and dire wolves, to the ultimate show of dominance – burning their lands and forcing them out so that we could repurpose it for our own wants and needs. It may be time to take a closer look at this dynamic. Evidence has been slowly accumulating that the other animals have had enough, that Mrs. O'Leary's cow was not an aberration but quite possibly the fore runner in a long line of animal arsonists seeking revenge. Judge for yourselves.

In 1871, Kate O'Leary kept five cows in a cramped barn in a busy section of Chicago. Now as far as we know, cows did not evolve for city living, but at least in India people have the good sense to let them wander the streets freely, sampling merchant's produce and fine fabrics as their tastes dictate, and they appear all the happier for it. Whether Mrs. O'Leary's cows knew anything about their free cousins in India is open to speculation, but the fire that resulted from one of them kicking over a lantern is not. The Great Chicago Fire killed 300 and left over a hundred thousand homeless. It also leveled 3.3 square miles, and the last chance cows in the U.S. would ever have to taste the free life of the city. That's no bull.

In separate incidents, two black bears in northern California demonstrated their fire starter capabilities in completely different ways. One showed the depth of its despair over recent human depredations in the area by climbing a utility pole and electrocuting itself, thereby initiating a wildfire that nearly caused people to think about the consequences of their actions. The people recovered, but the bear did not.

The other bear however took its issues right to The Man by jumping or falling from a rock cut above a road and right onto a passing police cruiser, which caused the car to crash and burn, igniting the roadside brush. Before he was sedated and taken to a nearby hospital for observation, the dazed officer swore he saw other bears high-fiving atop the rock cut. The offending bear ran off before it could be charged.

In London, England, a mouse that was clearly fed up with a woman who kept all her cheese in a tall, sealed box chewed the refrigerator's power cord and started a house fire from which only the cheese survived.

A beaver near Vancouver, Canada showed what it thought of humans turning trees into utility poles and stringing them through its cleared forest by dropping a real tree onto the power lines and starting a forest fire that burned for several days. Momentum there has been building in recent years to remove the beaver from its vaunted position as National Emblem and replace it with some sort of tree, of which Canada has so many that it really does justify the old folksy saying, "You can't throw a beaver around here without hitting a tree, hey?"

Birds may be the worst offenders in this burgeoning battle and yet somehow have managed to keep largely above suspicion. But they possibly have the most to lose as bird populations around the world have plummeted. Pigeons and sparrows in particular have wormed their way into such close proximity with humans as to be virtually unnoticeable, advance guard perhaps of a secret avian air force. Their battle plan is simplicity itself, picking up discarded, lit cigarette butts and depositing them in old attic or roof top nests. So many house, apartment, and store fires have resulted that one could almost think that birds are expecting a giant, vengeful Phoenix to rise from the ashes to lead them back to their rightful place in the world. (Needless to say, they are also not a big fan of vaping.)

And I challenge anyone to find a clearer, or dare I say more deserving case of retribution than the one that comes from an infuriated squirrel in South Dakota who took one vehicle off the road in spectacular fashion. Rather ingeniously it stockpiled pinecones in the engine compartment of the terminator machine, and one day as its owners were merrily driving the squirrel killing fields that are our public roadways, they caught fire and destroyed the vehicle. One down, 287 million to go.

More animals than I can recount here have picked up the torch, including pigs, geese, and even man's best friend. "Only YOU can prevent forest fires!" said a stern looking Smokey the Bear, speaking for all animals while pointing an accusatory finger at us humans. Little did we know it was all a ruse. It's time we pointed our fingers right back at them.

WHAT DO WE HAVE TO LOSE?

Some friends and I, all of a certain age, agree that the older we get the more we have the strange feeling that we've lost a part of ourselves. More than, say, our youth, which was a bit hard to take at first, or even our middle age, which was when it started to seem pretty clear that something nefarious was afoot. My wife's explanation that we'd all lost our minds didn't cut it. She's no scientist. I am, so mind or no mind, I decided to investigate further.

Well, it turns out we were both right. Apparently my brain is losing 60 neurons, or nerve cells, every minute. And with each passing year even more think, "What's the point?" Brain scientists say don't worry, the remaining cells have something they call plasticity, and can pick up the slack. Sounds nice, but I'm pretty sure brain cells don't like to work that hard on a good day. At least mine don't anyway. And now, just when old age has earned them an extra shot of dopamine, they're being told to work overtime? If that were the case I think we'd see more than 60 neurons per minute calling it quits, or at least threatening a strike over better working conditions.

Now brains are important, but it's not hard to find people without one, if we count people of different political parties, religious affiliations, or TV viewing habits from our own. But try imagining a person without skin! Every hour we lose 40,000 skin cells! And if that doesn't mean anything to you, that's 105 pounds of skin we lose by age 70! Almost enough to create another person if you save it, which you can't because it horrifically turns into all that dust you fastidiously wipe off your furniture! I could continue with more exclamations, but sensitive guy that I am, I wrote a poem to express my feelings instead:

> I watch the dust accumulate, All across my room,
> And have to think that at this rate, I'm watching my own doom.
> For dust, you see, is made of skin, At least that's what I'm hearing,
> So as it grows, to my chagrin, I fear I'm disappearing.

And no one has to tell me about the hair I'm losing, not if they don't want me to tell them they just lost a friend. It's hard enough looking into a mirror and trying to remember what 100,000 hairs looked like without learning that 40 -100 of the little traitors go AWOL every day, with more and more deciding never to return. I'm starting to wonder if this is a retaliation for shaving, which rather brutally slices a pound of hair off over 10 years, and haircuts, which chop a whopping 590 miles of hair off over a lifetime. Maybe it would help if I lost the mirror.

As if all this wasn't enough, most people lose half their taste buds by age 60. Where they go and why is a bit of a mystery. It could be because they've simply lost the will to go on, since the average 65 year old only has 2/3 of his or her teeth left, and those in a decidedly less than average condition, while 27% have had all their pearly whites head for the pearly gates. A steady diet of oatmeal after a lifetime of steak and corn on the cob could be enough to make any taste bud think twice about sticking around.

By the time we turn 70, each finger will have lost about 9 feet worth of nails to the clipper. Each toe, somewhat less. The amount of bodily fluids, associated byproducts, and intestinal gas manufactured and lost in the pursuit of longevity would fill a freight train, though finding an engineer to drive it could be a challenge. And last but not least, those disappearing brain cells I noted earlier not only take with them whatever sense we had, but also our senses. I've already mentioned taste, but our senses of sight, smell, touch, and hearing are also deserting us, slowly, like they think we won't notice. With both our sense and senses diminished, they may be right.

And speaking of senses, despite having already lost some parts of myself with which I was rather attached, I still have the foreboding sense that I could lose a lot more. Things like my will power for instance, or my self-respect. Recliners, heated car seats, and afternoon naps have been calling. Undoubtedly there are others. The more research I seem to do on this subject, the more worried I get. How can we ever win if we're always losing?

CONTEMPLATE THIS

The yogi, meditatively,
Closed his eyes to better see,
The truths his mind would find.

The tiger that crept up on him,
Cared only that his eyes were dim,
Not what his mind divined.

So the tiger ate the yogi raw,
But for the part he never saw,
And left his mind behind.

DON'T BELIEVE IT

The Yeti said to Bigfoot,
"Man, I think we should exist.
I think that humans actually should see us."

Then God appeared and scolded Yeti,
"Be a realist.
Only I have the omnipotence to free us."

"Not for nothing," countered Bigfoot,
"But I'm an atheist.
So I'd really rather be us than a Deus."

DO BIRDS THINK?

For some reason people think I have an answer to this question, just because I've written several essays about birds. And probably because these people know that the first rule of advice to writers is to write about what you know. Maybe it says something about me, or the quality of my education, but I think that is about the dumbest advice a writer could get. If I had to limit my writing to what I know, I'd never be able to pick up a pen. It might take some more work and imagination to write about what I don't know, but at least the field is wide open. And why should writers be singled out for this sort of advice anyway? I think talkers should also be included, as clearly most people don't know what they're talking about.

What I'm trying to say is that I don't know birds. Either personally, or as a Class. But where would I be if I let that stop me? I also write about the workings of my own mind, and I know even less about that. Frankly, I'm afraid to know more.

This question of birds thinking has flummoxed us as far back as Aristotle, who in 350 B.C., finally concluded in his *The History of Animals* that birds are not all that complex, only halfway on his scale between plants and humans. Personally, I don't think that Aristotle was all that complex, but what can you expect from someone who believed that the heart is the seat of reason? It kind of makes all his work suspect, don't you think?

I believe Aristotle was wrong about birds. I believe they do think. Modern scientists after all tend to say they are just as smart as they need to be. On second thought, I'm not quite sure how to take that statement. I remember that's what my parents would tell me after I would hear them talking about how smart other kids were.

The scientists do say though that just because birds don't have a neocortex doesn't mean they don't think. Now I may not be a bird brain scientist, but I don't think that statement can stand up to scrutiny. And not just by grammarians. Triple negative aside, even a neocortex doesn't seem to help a lot of people I know. Birds apparently do have a medial spiriform nucleus however, and more neurons per square inch than even primates. That's got to account for something, in spite of those scientists who say they have just as many neurons as they need to have. I'm starting to think that maybe we have more scientists than we need to have.

OK, I know what you're going to say. Why haven't birds figured out something as simple as windows then? To that I say give them time. How long did it take us to figure out flight, and that's a fair bit more complex than windows. Birds have been flying since Archaeopteryx decided that reptiles were for the birds 150 million years ago, while we didn't figure out windows until the early Romans finally concluded that they just couldn't see well through solid walls. Even then it took many bumps on Roman noggins to realize that, while windows were a marked improvement over wood and stone, they still couldn't just go and stick their heads outside any old time they wanted.

So it appears that scientists need more time too, in their case, to get to the bottom of this question about bird's thinking. To that end they continue to observe bird behaviors, conduct experiments, and dissect bird brains in an all-out effort to determine just how smart they are. Here are just a few examples of their findings:

- Pigeons can distinguish between the works of Picasso and Monet.
- Many birds use tools such as sticks and stones to help in obtaining food. New Caledonian crows will even improvise tools from objects they've never seen before.
- Ravens and magpies can identify themselves in a mirror. Primates are the only other animals that can do this.
- Crows leave walnuts in the street to let cars do their nut cracking for them.
- Many birds plan for hard times by caching food. A Clark's nutcracker can remember where it stored over 3,000 pieces of food, even under a cover of snow.
- Parrots are able to understand the meaning of words, and even to create simple sentences.
- Many birds can find their way home after migrating thousands of miles. Scientists even moved a flock of white-crowned sparrows 3,000 miles to

unfamiliar territory and watched them make a beeline back.
- Crows can hold grudges for years against people who have treated them badly, and even warn their friends and family about them.
- Scientists probably think that this means they're getting somewhere with all this research. Birds probably think that scientists have experimented on them long enough, and that scientists are just as smart as they need to be.

TAKE YOUR MIND FOR A WALK

As I was out walking the other day, the thought occurred to me that many interesting thoughts occur to me while I'm out walking. Like the one about how our ancestors came down from the trees some four million or so years ago and took up walking for the first time. And how this might have been when they took up thinking for the first time also. It's hard to know for sure as paleontologists have yet to discover any fossilized thoughts. My wife says that's only because they haven't studied any of mine.

Thoughts like these, I've learned, would likely never have even happened if our arboreal ancestors hadn't taken that first giant step for mankind to begin with. This is because, studies have shown, walking improves one's creative thinking. Even my wife, who has been studying me for years, concluded that my thinking is never more creative than when I come back from a walk knowing there's a list of chores waiting for me.

Those early walkers had to get creative in a hurry of course, and may have sensed that their kind would never live to pass down their interesting thoughts if they didn't quickly show how creative they could get. So after it became painfully clear that they lacked the claws and fangs that many other ground dwellers had, they invented running. This had the effect of improving their creative thinking further, and so with their newly freed hands, they began to pick up sticks and stones and invented weapons. While this allowed them to slow back down to a walk, mankind really hit the fast track now.

With the creativity of those early walkers unleashed, language was invented and fire was domesticated. Impressive accomplishments unquestionably, but where would those early walkers really have gotten to without the shoe? The shoe provided comfort, and allowed the walker to travel great distances, opening up the world as it opened the walkers' minds. It's rather surprising though that the oldest shoe discovered only dates back 10,000 years. Personally, I would have thought that "I need shoes!" would have been among the first things uttered after language was invented. We'll never know, as the list of things humans needed was still rather long at this point, and with writing not invented until 3400 BC, they couldn't very well have kept a written to-do list.

What's still more surprising is that it took until 1790 to invent shoelaces! And not until 1818 were shoes differentiated for the right and left feet! I think these shortcomings can be laid directly at the feet of horses. Horse riding was discovered 5,000 years ago, which began to take mankind off its own feet and off its creative game. Horseshoes, which were invented 2500 years ago, didn't need laces, and the same shoe worked just fine for the right, left, front, and back feet. Maybe we should be thankful that our shoes aren't nailed on.

Fortunately, the greatest walkers stayed on their feet, and proved to be the greatest minds. From Socrates and Aristotle, to Beethoven, Darwin, and Einstein, walkers such as these consistently proved Friedrich Nietzsche's maxim, "All truly great thoughts are conceived while walking." Modern studies have confirmed this, showing that people think best when walking at 3 miles per hour. Caution must be advised however. It has also been reported that walkers approaching thinking speeds of 10 thoughts per hour dramatically increase their odds of an accident involving a tree or a cliff.

The great thinker Jean-Jacques Rousseau claimed that walking saved his life. It also killed him when he was run over by a horse and carriage, giving us the first early warning about distracted walking. We don't know what he was thinking at the time, but odds are it was somewhere between one of his greatest thoughts and "Sacre-Bleu!"

Unfortunately, the popularity of the horse and carriage was the beginning of the end for the everyday walker, and the everyday thinker wasn't far behind. Walking and thinking take up a great store of the body's available energy, so it proved very attractive for most people to ride and talk instead. Neither of those activities took any energy, and could be done by non-thinkers from all walks of life.

So the wheel, one of mankind's greatest inventions in 3400 BC, was back, and soon it was poised to put even the horse out of business. The bicycle, the train, and the horseless carriage, or automobile, followed, taking ever more people off their feet. The creativity of the modern walkers/thinkers, people like Steve Jobs and Mark Zuckerberg, still shined, but at what cost? Nowadays, most modern walkers are unthinking smart phone users who can't walk across the street without texting, or listening to music or podcasts. Why strain your own brain when you can carry one with you? Serious injuries and deaths to distracted walkers are increasing yearly at the hands of equally distracted drivers.

As walking has become a life-threatening activity once again, distracted thinking has prevailed. This is not a recipe for the advancement of mankind, and neither running nor weapons can help us this time. The latest thought I had while I was out walking was that humans are devolving. If we all don't start taking walking seriously again, and soon, we might all be driven back into the trees from whence we came. How's that for creative thinking?

THE DIRT ON
FOREST BATHING

Have you ever experienced a feeling of solitude when you're alone in the woods? No? Well don't feel alone here either. If you're like most people, when you're alone in the woods all you feel is panic, because you would never intentionally be alone in the woods in the first place. It's like that feeling you get at night when you're watching TV in bed and the power goes out. Your imagination is suddenly released into a dark and frightening new environment, and as if it knows it will be shackled again soon enough, it flies every which way shouting about all the unseen dangers that are closing in on you at that very moment.

That's no way to feel friluftsliv, or waldeinsamkeit either, for that matter. Those are Norwegian and German words for just such a feeling of sylvan solitude, words which frankly scare the bejeesus out of me even more than being alone in the woods. Which is what brings me to Japan's answer to all this woodsy worry. They call it shin-rin-yoku, and have the consideration to break a word like that up into bite size pieces so you can take it as slow and easy as you like. In English, it means forest bathing, a phrase that makes me feel clean all over just saying it. The Japanese define it is a deliberate, meditative engagement of all the senses while immersed in nature, and they should know. There isn't much left of nature in Japan, so it's understandable they would try to get as much out of it as they can.

If you're feeling any immersion apprehension however, you may find it soothing to know that the Forest Therapy Society is ready and waiting with trained and certified guides to show anyone so inclined the forest bathing experiences they've been missing, so that they might enjoy the stress relief and other health benefits the forest provides. Sounds nice, as far as it goes, which I'm sorry to say is only to the end of that sentence. Especially when they further define their mission as a way to develop a relationship of reciprocity with the forest, in which the wholeness and wellness of both the forest and the practitioner is supported. Personally, I believe the FTS has either gone and climbed out on a rotten limb, or they can't see the trees for the forest, because it's that statement that cannot be supported. They completely fail to explain what the forest gets out of this arrangement.

Now I may be more a TV guide than a forest guide kind of person, but even I can recognize human exploitation when it's eighty feet tall and covers more ground than a shopping mall. Schopenhauer said, 'It is only when he is alone that a man is really free,' and I think he meant it, whether a forest was involved or not. But I think it was Muir, not Schopenhauer or the FTS who thought of the trees when he said, 'It is only when a forest is left alone that the trees are really free.' All across the globe forests have been chopped down or burned alive to make room for humans, and if anything is in need of therapy here it's the forests. Talk about stress! The only sense they likely engage when humans are near is the sense of impending doom.

Now I know the FTS is not malicious, and forest bathing does sound wonderful, but couldn't they have left it at tree hugging? Change the name to the Tree Therapy Society, and sincerely appreciate the trees as individuals, and maybe then they can talk about reciprocity. Till then, I'm thinking that the forests would prefer that we all do our bathing in the lakes. They shouldn't have to witness such things. Their stress levels are eighty feet high as it is.

PARENTING, A TERRIFYING VOYAGE INTO THE UNKNOWN

Procreation – where would we be without it? But to suggest, as the word implies, that creation is a job for the pros, is to overlook the fact that rank amateurs have been at it from the very beginning. No apprenticeships, training, or certificates required. One need not look any further for confirmation of this than at the bewildered and overwhelmed parents who find themselves suddenly alone with a helpless bundle of joy and terror, and no off switch at any end. Trial and error is the only rule book for these amateurs, and error never had it so good. But not even this can deter prospective parents from procreating. They have a greater purpose in mind, and though it may be in the far back of their minds, who needs a plan when you have a purpose?

What no parent actually acknowledges, and what children don't realize, is that the purpose of parents is quite simple. It is none other than to create a replica of themselves. What more lofty, God-like goal could there be than to create life in one's own perfect image? As there are generally two parents involved however, this goal immediately becomes problematic, and is the source of much conflict to the child caught in the crossfire.

Additionally, what no parent actually acknowledges, and what children don't realize, is that once a child changes into a teenager the purpose of a parent also changes. The once lofty goal of self-replication will have been thrown out the window in favor of the distinctly more basic one of self-preservation. This is best exemplified by the typically unspoken questions that go through most parent's minds, such as "What the hell have I created?" "Who is this person living with me?" and "What if he becomes a serial killer, lawyer, or member of the wrong political party, and society blames me?" The motivation for this sudden change in purpose of course is fear.

Fear is one of the biggest motivating factors there is, and a fear of the unknown is an especially virulent form. And who can truly know a teenager? This is what is particularly terrifying to the parent. To raise a child from a newborn baby is to know everything that can be known about another human. And to suddenly have that hard won satisfaction, security, and yes, self-reflected image taken from a parent and replaced with a stranger, and a stranger that intentionally and systematically undermines all that careful early crafting of a replicate human being to boot, causes many parents to begin to experience frightening new nightmares of alien abductions. If the known can turn into the unknown right before one's eyes, what can truly ever be known about the world?

DANCING TO YOUR CIRCADIAN RHYTHM

"Early to bed and early to rise, makes a man healthy, wealthy, and wise," Ben Franklin famously said in 1735. Ben, it would seem, was a morning person. Of course this was way back before electric lights and smartphones, so everyone was forced by necessity to be morning people. Night people would have been left alone in the dark with their own minds, which has never been such a wise or healthy thing. But how are the morning larks and the night owls faring in the 21st century, now that the science vultures have had a chance to pick their lives apart?

It doesn't take an ornithologist to tell the difference between larks and owls. Most of us who are one or the other know that it usually doesn't go so well when we lose the beat of our Circadian rhythm, the biological clock that governs our personal sleep patterns, as well as our metabolism, brain activity, and a host of other bodily functions I didn't even know were on our dance cards. While the larks songs often turn into snores much past sunset, the world still runs on daylight time. This means that the world gets the benefit of their peak performances, and leaves the owls to fight against their innate sleep timing in order to fit in. This primordial battle between darkness and light can cause the owls more problems than an alarm clock and a Starbucks barista can fix.

Studies show that night owls, for instance, are much more prone to bad habits like smoking and drinking. This is not so surprising given that the focus of the daylight hours is on business, while the focus of the night is on forgetting business. Unless we're talking about monkey business, as night owls are significantly more likely to close on their romantic deals. It is probably slight consolation to the early birds that they get the worms.

Larks generally need less sleep, and sleep more soundly, with light, fantastical dreams that entertain and amuse. So it's easy to see how they wake up refreshed and ready to annoy the hell out of the night owls, who are more apt to sleep at work because they are also more apt to work at sleep. Insomnia and sleep apnea are not uncommon with them, and I'd rather watch a horror movie alone than ask a night owl about his or her dreams.

As if all this wasn't enough to cause night owls to sit out the dance, studies show that they are more prone to depression and obesity, and that larks are more persistent, cooperative, conscientious, and proactive. And they procrastinate less. To top it off, they may be happier, as the old expression, "Happy as a lark," suggests. Of course, clams are supposed to be a benchmark for happiness also, and I've never seen a clam sing or dance, so maybe I should stick to the current studies instead of the old expressions.

Then again, the "wise owls" may just have the studies to back up that expression, as the night owls outperformed the morning larks in intelligence tests. And to rub it in, they even did it in the morning, likely with one eye closed and brains that were foggier than London in the springtime. Perhaps associated with this finding, researchers also discovered that night owls generally have larger incomes, although much of it may go towards coffee and therapists.

It seems then that old Ben Franklin liked a good joke, for he must have not only been early to rise, but late to bed also. A morning lark AND a night owl, with a little afternoon mockingbird thrown in for good measure. How else to explain a man who was a writer, publisher, politician, philosopher, postmaster, scientist, inventor, Freemason, humorist, musician, statesman, activist, diplomat, ladies' man, father of three, and Founding Father of our country. Perhaps he never slept. Circadian rhythms aside, he certainly danced to his own beat. For the rest of us mortals however, be we larks or owls, it would seem that the trifecta of health, wealth, and wisdom is only a dream. Which is why I'm going back to bed.

IT'S YOUR FAULT

For a very long time,
The primordial slime,
Was all that ever existed.

But then something stirred,
And a life form occurred,
And one day crawled out unassisted.

And I know it seems weird,
But that life persevered,
And eventually resulted in you.

But don't get a big head,
For I recently read,
The results are under review.

DIVIDED WE STAND

The amoeba dad said, "I need to split!"
The mom said, "Not without me!"
"Though I kind of like it here too," he admit.
"It's our destiny," said she.

"Divided we stand, united we fall,
That's the amoeba way.
Why don't you see we can have it all
By getting to both go and stay."

THINGS

Things could be better,
Things could be worse.
They might be a blessing,
They could be a curse.
They might tie us up,
Or they could set us free.
But if it weren't for things,
Then where would we be?

THE AGE OF DOGS

The secret to how humans age has long been one of the great mysteries of science. Now, in a new study that may or may not have any significance on this at all, scientists working on The Dog Aging Project are hoping to gain insight on human aging by monitoring 10,000 pet dogs over their lifetime. The dogs, who are ensured proper nutrition and medical care, are fine with this, but there are many humans who think that a Human Aging Project that provides proper nutrition and medical care to all humans would be more appropriate.

The reason scientists are interested in studying dogs is because they have a lot in common with humans, and not just those humans who are always in the doghouse for inappropriate behavior. Dogs live in the same environment as humans, and also suffer from many of the same health problems, such as arthritis, obesity, and diabetes. A significant difference though is that many of their problems cannot be blamed on excessive smoking, drinking, or TV watching. Sadly, some are incorrigible. On the other hand, their predilection for eating things best left on the lawn cannot be a recipe for healthy aging. We all hope so anyway.

One particular mystery that has long eluded scientists is why small dogs tend to live a lot longer than large dogs. Recently however, researchers in Germany have determined that a dog's life expectancy is reduced by about a month for every 4.4 pounds of body mass. There is no word yet on whether or not the scientists engaged on The Dog Aging Project either concur with this finding or judge it to have any significance on human aging, as they have been quite busy with their new diet plans.

Dogs age much faster than humans, which is another reason for this study. The scientists can study 7 – 10 dogs in the time it would take them to study one human. Their strategy is already paying dividends in the form of at least one consequential new discovery, that of calculating your dog's age in human years. Simply multiplying by 7 will no longer do. Now you will need to either be a math whiz or have advanced calculator training, as the new, improved formula is to multiply the natural logarithm of the dog's age by 16, and then add 31. I know what you're thinking. Most of us will have aged many years before we ever figure out what a logarithm is, and I'm betting that when we do, we will discover that there is nothing natural about it.

This new method of figuring a dog's age comes from researchers who examine the chemical changes that occur to DNA over time. These changes apparently don't alter the content of the genes themselves, only their activity levels. It is these gene activity levels that primarily interest them. The scientists hope that by studying them it will help in developing what they call an epigenetic clock that reveals not only how fast a dog is aging, but why. This, of course, could have enormous potential for those humans who wish to have a clock instead of a mirror to tell them how fast they're aging.

On the plus side, one thing I've learned about this new dog aging formula is that it means a dog ages slower as it gets older. For instance, a 2 year old dog under the old rule would be a 14 year old teenager in the prime of its youth, whereas now it would be 42 and wondering what happened. By 5, instead of 35, it would be 56 ¾. But by 10, the formula really starts to work to a dog's advantage. Instead of 70, it would be just 67.8. As an aging human, I like where this might be going. In the ultimate race against the clock, there are no winners, but I'd be happy to discover that I'm a slow loser.

While aging so far still remains a mystery, dogs are not. They have been with us for at least 20,000 years, asking so little of us in return for their unwavering companionship and emotional support. This can be no better epitomized than by the saying, "A dog is man's best friend." The scientists in The Dog Aging Project understand this, and ultimately hope that the study of these 10,000 dogs will enable us to be better friends to dogs, by uncovering the secrets that will allow us to extend their lives. And eventually, if these secrets are also found to apply to humans, we'll have 10,000 more reasons to appreciate dogs, and more time to show it.

BOREDOM – IT'S NOT JUST FOR THE BORING

"A subject for a great poet would be God's boredom after the seventh day of creation." So mused the existentialist philosopher Frederick Nietzsche, whose discursive, tortuous philosophy books did their best to give readers a glimpse into that state of being. Nietzsche was strongly influenced on the subject by the philosopher Arthur Schopenhauer, who, in one of his cheerier moments, wrote that "Life swings like a pendulum between pain and boredom." (And I thought we were doing a rather good job of keeping God amused. Or angry. Anything but bored.) They say that everybody gets bored, but if you're not too bored to read more about it, stay with me, and stay clear of philosophy books. They didn't seem to do poor Schopenhauer much good.

No one is more of a present day expert on boredom than John Eastwood, director of The Boredom Lab at York University in Toronto. (I've heard that this campus is also home to The Apathy Lab, The Inertia Workshop, and The Dullness Center, so a breakthrough is bound to come any day from YU. YU? Why me?) John would be more of an expert if his assistants weren't so prone to staring into space, doodling, and contemplating their navels. (How do you think you would fare if your job was to use various statistical methods such as hierarchical linear modeling and structural equation modeling to deepen our understanding of boredom?)

Still, Eastwood has managed to debunk the popular notion that only boring people get bored, by discovering that other personality types also suffer from boredom. An example is the impulsive person who is always looking for new and exciting experiences, and as a result is chronically under-stimulated. This type has been known to wear out TV remotes at twice the average rate. (It should be noted though that boring people resent the intrusion into what had previously been considered their exclusive domain.) Perhaps Eastwood was on to something when he also stated that boredom is a crisis in meaning. (I have no idea what that means, but I wouldn't yet call it a crisis, although I did yawn when I read it.)

Some psychologists believe that boredom is a trait, which is what non-psychologists call a characteristic, or an aspect, or a feature. Many of these people call psychologists other names as well. Some people get excited when they learn that psychologists can now measure their boredom. (The people's boredom, not the psychologists. Theirs is a given. Imagine if YOU had to listen to people's problems all day long.) The Boredom Proneness Scale measures one's propensity to feel bored by asking a series of 28 questions. I'll bet that all you non-psychologists could think of just one question that would have done the trick, but then there's all that grant money to consider. The Multidimensional State Boredom Scale measures the state of one's feelings of boredom in any given situation, and from many different dimensions, including the one that psychologists inhabit. More specific boredom scales include the Job Boredom Scale, the Leisure Boredom Scale, and the Spousal Boredom Scale, although no one in their right mind would bring that last one up without having a lawyer on standby.

Philosophers and psychologists alike agree that boredom is a modern luxury, nonexistent until the late 18th century as the Enlightenment ceded to the Industrial Revolution. Before this, survival took precedence, and staring into space was decidedly not much of a survival skill then. It took the TV to change all that. But now that it's here, many experts say that we should embrace boredom as the think tank of the soul, and look at it as a positive force; a call to action or an opportunity for thought and reflection. Of course if all you can think about is getting back to the TV, perhaps your first step should be either towards Eastwood's lab or a wilderness survival experience, because if one's boredom is too luxurious it can lead to despair, especially with what TV has to offer these days.

Don't listen to me, listen to the philosophers again. I don't think it's my imagination that picks up the despair in their voices. Soren Kierkegaard said both that, "People settle for a level of despair they can tolerate and call it happiness," and, "Boredom is the root of all evil – a fear of oneself." His brother in boredom, Schopenhauer, said, "Boredom is merely the feeling of the emptiness of life." Before you say that those guys should have gotten out more, hear first from Susan Ertz, who said, "Millions long for immortality who don't know what to do with themselves on a rainy Sunday afternoon." (I don't think Ms. Ertz was technically a philosopher because that statement is a bit too funny if you ask me.)

As for me, I prefer to take my philosophical and motivational guidance from Winnie the Pooh, who said, "People say that nothing is impossible, but I do nothing every day." I don't know what the philosophers and psychologists would say about that, but I couldn't be bored less.

WATCH OUT FOR NIGHT WATCHMEN

Just who are the night watchmen, and why would anybody ever want a job patrolling the dark grounds of commercial, industrial, and military installations when they could be safe in bed with only dark dreams to trouble them. What do we know of these people who watch the night, and get paid to do it? And what's wrong with their other senses?

The night, after all, is ruled by the moon, La Luna, Goddess of lunatics everywhere, and influencer of such strange mysteries as tides, gravity, love, werewolves, late night TV programming, and of course conspiracy theories. It also happens to be the peculiar domain of night watchmen, late night radio talk show ranters, and anti-social loners with psychopathic tendencies. It is not a domain for the faint of heart, or the weak of mind. Or for that matter, the jaundiced of liver, given the outsized part that alcohol often has to play. Conspiracy theories are like mother's milk to these people, if mother's milk was a government brainwashing plot to shove socialism and a liberal agenda down a helpless baby's throat.

Even early humans learned pretty quickly that it made no sense to watch the night. For one thing, you couldn't see much. Not like in the daylight when you could see the cave bear or the saber-toothed tiger stalking you. Nighttime was for laying low, for hiding even, and for scary stories around the fire about the unseen dangers that stalked the incautious and the over-confident alike.

To venture into the night was to ignore the protective spirits of the light and show just how helpless we are without them. A person in the dark was as directionless as a blindfolded teenager, and if such a person came back at all, they would have come back a profoundly changed person. They would have been full of crazy stories and conspiracy theories about a dark, dangerous world that only they knew, the first of the late-night talk show ranters. Most early humans would have had to find the courage to move deeper into the cave, to get further away from both the night and the ranter. Just to be safe.

Modern humans just need to find the courage to change the radio station. Or to get another job.

WORLD MIGRATORY BIRD DAZE

If it appears to you that the days have been flying by lately, it could just be an illusion. Especially if you're exhausted from celebrating World Migratory Bird Day on the second Saturday of May, a time of year already crowded with such fun times as the always crazy No Socks Day and the quirkily charming National Hamster day.

This is because there is another World Migratory Bird Day fast approaching on the second Saturday of October, when we will have another, hopefully calmer, chance to commemorate the achievements of these remarkable birds. The only serious competition then is World Egg Day, but this is easily dismissed as there would be no eggs to celebrate if it weren't for birds. At least not the kind worthy of our attention. You may argue that chickens aren't migratory birds. I would suggest that we let them out of their cages and let them have the last word on that.

Forty percent of the world's birds migrate, so clearly this is not some passing fad. These birds were born into the life of a migrant, with all the baggage that comes with it. At certain times every year, whether they like it or not, hormonal changes cause most to enter a state called hyperphagia. This is not a state for the faint hearted, and if you should ever find yourself approaching it, look for detour signs. This state triggers a feeding frenzy to make pigs unworthy of the name, as well as restless flying and flock gathering behaviors. And not just the teenagers. Many birds, like the blackpoll warbler for instance, gain twice their weight in a few short weeks. It is enough to make one wonder if body shaming by non-migratory birds is really behind this frantic urge to hit the open skies.

Birds that don't migrate are called sedentary birds, and are rightly ridiculed for their provincial attitudes and uptight natures. It could be the reason for there being no World Sedentary Bird Day. They are simply uninteresting birds, and the less said about them the better. Not one of them can compare to the daredevil feats of the Ruppel's griffon vulture, the highest flyer on record. It was unfortunate that to get into the record books one had to get sucked into the engine of a plane flying at 37,000 feet, but maybe it thought no one would believe it otherwise. The pilot was astounded, but the rest of the Ruppel's griffon vulture community reacted predictably by yawning and sticking their heads back into the carcasses of dead animals.

The bar-tailed godwit flies 7000 miles in eight days, without stopping. It tries to lord that performance over the other birds when it finally lands, but it's a bar-tailed godwit, so no one pays it any attention. The arctic tern, whose yearly trips from the Arctic to the Antarctic and back put 49,700 miles on its odometer, puts the bar-tailed godwit to shame. Added up over its average lifespan of 30 years, that's 1.5 million miles, all so it can enjoy two summers per year. Still, the summers are in the Arctic and the Antarctic. Someone ought to tell them that they fly right over the likes of Rio and Hawaii. And in case you were wondering, experts remain undecided about whether its distant relative the wandering albatross actually migrates or merely pretends to.

The great snipe is the fastest migrating bird, flying 4,700 miles at 60 mph. It is listed as near threatened. Just imagine how fast it could fly if it was truly threatened. The ruby-throated hummingbird is the smallest migrating bird, flying 900 miles over the Caribbean Sea in 20 hours. It is not threatened, but like all hummingbirds, tends to act like it is because of its size.

The short-tailed shearwater, aka the Tasmanian mutton bird, is a species known locally as flying sheep by the Australians who commercially harvest them for their feathers, flesh, and oil. Still other names for them are yolla and moon bird. It is one thing to prey on defenseless nesting birds, but to call them names on top of it is unforgivable. It is probably the reason why their migratory journey takes them so far from home – to remote Kamchatka in the Russian far east, then to the Aleutian Islands, then around the whole Pacific Ocean. Not being one of our smarter birds, it mistakes so much plastic garbage for food on its journey that it dies in great numbers. Unless it prefers to die this way rather than at the hands of the insensitive Australians.

So the next time you use that awful avian insult and say that something is "for the birds", remember that there are two World Migratory Bird Days. What other person, animal, or object can claim such a tribute?

THE PURSUIT OF HAPPINESS CAN LEAVE YOU EXHAUSTED

It makes me unhappy to think that our Founding Fathers may have misled us when they proclaimed in the Declaration of Independence our unalienable right to pursue happiness. Not to possess it, just to pursue it. The statement seems to imply that happiness is either an unattainable quest, like immortality, or the perfect beer, or might only be achieved by chasing it down and pouncing on it like a greased pig. At best then, happiness itself would seem to be a slippery proposition, and probably not for everybody. I mean, how many people would be happy with a greased pig?

One could, I suppose, alternatively interpret the statement to mean that it is the very pursuit of happiness that could make us happy. That happiness is a journey, not a destination. I confess I do find the idea of a bus full of happy people on a trip to nowhere an intriguing one. And I don't think it's just because I have an unfair advantage here, given that people have been telling me that I've been headed nowhere for years. No, I think it's as much about all the happy people you'd be surrounded by that makes the difference. Somehow if you're only surrounded by unhappy whiners even a trip to Tahiti will bring you down.

This would seem to bring up two problems that I can see – where to find Happy People to surround yourself with, and where do you go with them, because even if you're on a journey to nowhere you have to stop and refuel now and then. Or work, pay the bills, and do all the other things that make so many people unhappy. Unless, claims Eric Weiner, author of "The Geography of Bliss," you head for Iceland. I suppose that makes some sense. If you've got to be somewhere, Iceland's about as close to nowhere as you can get.

Now I know Iceland might seem like the last place you'd expect to find Happy People, but no less an authority than Ruut Veenhoven, the 'Happiness Professor' himself and founder of the World Database of Happiness, says that Iceland leads the world in happiness. And not just the bottled variety, though apparently Icelanders do get as thirsty as the next country. As long as the next country's not at the bottom of the happiness rankings, like Moldova or Russia, and full of professional drinkers on the unhappy bus to despair and hopelessness. Those are two stops you definitely want to avoid.

By contrast, Weiner says that Icelanders, whose country, by the way, is perpetually threatened by volcanoes, earthquakes, frigid cold, and a sun that would rather be someplace else, seem to thrive on nature's sense of impending doom. I bet apocalyptic bedtime stories for children are big sellers there too. One of their secrets is the philosophy that, "If you are not happy, you had better stop worrying about it and see what treasures you can pluck from your own brand of unhappiness." It seems to fall a little short somehow, but what do I know. My own country's not about to fall off the map at any moment.

The apocalypse equals happiness equation aside, the journal Psychological Science reports that if you're looking for Happy People, look at their genes, because studies show that happiness is 50% inherited. That at least should take some of the pressure off trying to be happy if you're not. Blaming your ancestors should help with the rest. But if you're still committed to pursuing happiness despite having genes that would be more comfortable in Moldova, the other 50% is still in play, and apparently might be found amongst your family, friends, faith, and work. I say might, because caution is advised if you need to inform any of these groups to pick up the slack. They have the ability to show you new levels of unhappiness that you hadn't seen before.

If a half ration of happiness doesn't sound so appealing to you, there might be another way to the whole enchilada. And you won't have to swap out your family, get on a bus to nowhere, or chase a greased pig to get it. You just need to sit still, because according to Nathaniel Hawthorne, "Happiness is a butterfly, which, when pursued, is always just beyond your grasp, but which, if you will sit down quietly, may alight upon you." This makes me believe that our Founding Fathers definitely didn't think this 'pursuit of happiness' thing through. What they should have given us is the unalienable right to wait as long as we want for the butterfly of happiness to bring it to us. That seems more appropriate somehow for a country that's only threatened by the amount of time it spends on the couch watching television.

WHO'S WINNING?

Tornadoes, typhoons,
Famines and floods,
Volcanoes, wildfires,
And landslides of mud.

Tsunamis and sinkholes,
Avalanches of snow,
Lightning above,
And earthquakes below.

Unholy heat waves,
Merciless drought,
While pestilence threatens
The world throughout.

If you're still not afraid
Life could end in a flash,
Think of comets and meteors
Or an asteroid crash.

As the earth tries to kill us
(And we've not seen its worst,)
We must try even harder
To kill the earth first.

BONSAI - THE ABHORRENT, YET ARTFUL, WAR ON TREES

Paleobotanists tell us that trees have been around in one form or another for 385 million years. They have appeared in small forms which some people have mistaken for shrubs, usually by crass, insensitive people who never apologized, and they have appeared in forms over three hundred feet high and wide enough to drive a bus through, which crass, insensitive people have. Perhaps they were the same people.

One form they definitely did not take though in all that time is the bonsai form. History will not look kindly on the deliberately hurtful people who came along and thought up that particularly heinous form of tree abuse. For those of you who don't know, bonsai is when you take a young tree which is destined to grow sixty or more feet and you subject it to drastic pruning, root reduction, potting in an undersized container, defoliation, wiring, clamping, and grafting in order to create a tiny tree that is a mere wisp of the tree it was intended to be. But still perfectly proportional. It was probably developed by people whose minds were not allowed to grow to the sizes they were intended to be.

Then to rub it in, these tree abusers call themselves artists, who say they do it for its calming, meditative effect. They would. I've heard that medieval torturers called themselves care givers, and believed that they were actually helping people to forget the hunger, disease, and war that plagued their stressful lives. But even they never thought of torturing trees, at least not beyond cutting them down, chopping them up, and setting them on fire so that they could burn people at the stake more effectively.

If bonsai sounds remarkably like Banzai!, the Japanese war cry that brought instant terror to all who heard it, it is undoubtedly intentional. Bonsai may have originated in China, where it was called penzai, but it was perfected by the Japanese. It is nothing less than a war on trees, albeit a very small war. But Japan is a small country, with small people. No need for big n'tall stores there. So a small war on trees would be fitting, and befitting the passive-aggressive nature of a people who torture larger visitors with capsule hotel rooms, tiny cars, mini meals, and even the world's smallest toilet.

This abuse of trees must stop. Trees are peaceful, sentient beings that are home to birds and beasts alike. Humans too have long sought refuge in their cool shade, or enjoyed climbing in their welcoming branches. Their sheer size and amazing longevity give them an unrivaled majesty. It is all stripped away by selfish, hurtful bonsai "artists" seeking inner calm. In my opinion, it would be a better world with more agitated artists and less trees that a bird couldn't land in without crushing.

DIY BRAIN ZAPPING

I confess that in the past I've done a bit of whining about the potential of the human brain. But that was before I heard about tDCS, otherwise known as transcranial Direct Current Stimulation. (I suppose the t is not capitalized because transcranial is an imposing, even intimidating word, and should be said softly and respectfully, at least until one gets comfortable with it.) Reference sites describe tDCS as a non-invasive procedure wherein one receives a small direct electrical current to the head via carefully placed electrodes in order to change neuron excitability and bring about alterations or improvements to brain function. Just in case your neurons aren't excited enough.

These changes could come in many forms, such as improvements to memory, problem solving, math and language skills, socialization, and attention span, or in the elimination of risk-taking behaviors and addictive cravings. You might think I'd follow all this up by saying, 'But don't try this at home', when in fact you can now purchase tDCS kits intended for home use, complete with electrode montages so you don't mistakenly forget the math you laboriously learned or acquire a smoking habit.

Unknown to me, scientists and doctors have long been intrigued by the possibility of using electricity to boost brain power. The ancient Roman Empire physician Galen experimented with putting electric fish on patient's heads to sometimes miraculous effect. One patient reportedly came in complaining of weight loss caused by a sudden, unexplainable aversion to food, and left desiring fish fried crisp in oil.

As you might imagine however, this treatment didn't really progress. I suspect it had to be pretty difficult to keep a fish on a patient's head for any appreciable length of time without either the fish dying of asphyxiation or the patient dying of humiliation. Also, I suspect a patient would have strongly objected to keeping his head in contact with the fish while it was in the fish's preferred medium. (As a side note, Galen was physician to the insane Roman emperor Commodus, who believed himself the God Hercules. Electric fish however were never directly implicated in his condition.)

Mary Shelley, in her book Frankenstein, brought the title character to life with electricity, thereby initiating about as big an improvement in mental capacity as one could hope, regardless of his math and language deficiencies. Later on though, the practice of applying repeated electrical charges to the head became associated with inducing catatonia in patients with severe psychiatric disorders. It sounds barbaric, I know. I could be wrong, but I'm thinking that's where the word revolting originated.

In more modern times the U.S. Department of Defense has reportedly experimented with tDCS in their attempts to create improved soldiers. As with their experiments with mind altering drugs however, results are classified. In this era of home kits and head-zapping amateurs, that is unfortunate, for there is still much to learn. But maybe it is intentional. Maybe the DOD is behind the dissemination of these kits, and is anticipating a surge in enlistments due to the creation of home-grown soldiers. It might be something to think about, before you put those electrodes on your noggin and try to give your neurons something to get excited about besides another weekend trip to the mall.

Anyway, this history is merely intended to inject a note of caution into the natural desire to improve one's mind. A centimeter off an electrode placement, a milliamp difference in the electrical current, a deviation of mere seconds in the time of current application – all contribute to the success or failure of the DIYer. It's tempting to think that by zapping my dorsolateral prefrontal cortex I can not only improve my memory, but quit smoking. On the other hand, I've apparently gotten along reasonably well so far with an underachieving dorsolateral prefrontal cortex. And with my tendency to overdo a good thing, I'd be concerned that a volt jolt could give me completely new memories, or cause my head to begin smoking.

And don't get me started on the inevitable future of wireless, remote-controlled brain zapping. If you think the nightly battle for control of the TV remote is bad, just imagine when you and your partner have the remotes to control each other's brains.

IN YOUR FACE

I can barely stand to say this, much less write about it, but I think it's fair to warn you that our faces are infested with mites. There, I said it. I stumbled across this unnerving information in the reputable magazine where I read it, and thought it my duty to pass it along.

It gets better. These mites are microscopic critters with eight legs that burrow headfirst into our pores and stay there for the rest of their lives. Scientists don't know why they do this, though it seems pretty clear to me they do it because they are ashamed of their own behavior and can't look us in the face. At least not in the proper fashion. Of course it also means that at any given moment there are hundreds of thousands of these disgusting things waving their asses at us every time we look in the mirror. Ha! Fooled you. They don't have anuses. Thank God for small favors, but this does raise a few other questions.

It gets better still. These critters are arachnids, which means they're in the spider and tick family. If that was my family, I would have run away at a very early age, for nothing good ever comes of it. Case in point – at night while we sleep, hundreds of thousands of these mites gather at our pore's openings – and have sex! Right there on our faces! Now I hate to criticize a whole species because of their loose morals, especially when scientists don't fully understand their lives or their family dynamics, but c'mon! Where are their parents?

And speaking of scientists again, what kind of respectable scientist would study face mites when there is no shortage of decent, wholesome animals to study? And then go and publish the results of their studies in respectable magazines for any unsuspecting reader to trip over. Where were these scientists parents when they needed them?

Well, at this point the cat is out of the bag. I suggest we drop the whole thing and go on with our lives as if microscopic, orgiastic, feces bloated spider-like monstrosities were not infesting every pore of our faces for reasons we don't understand.

GOOD COMPANY FOR ENDANGERED ANIMALS

I was thinking the other day about the start of the baseball season, and naturally it led me to the topic of endangered animals. (There might have been a few steps in-between, but I don't remember what they were.) Animals on the verge of extinction, to my way of thinking, should be on everyone's minds. How would you like it if your family was living on the cusp of oblivion and no one cared? I thought so.

Like the slow loris, the lesser Madagascar hedgehog tenrec, the blue-footed booby, and the honest politician, these fellow denizens of our fair earth are clearly lacking the physical or psychological attributes to adapt to a changing world. I know we shouldn't criticize, and what's past is past, but it might have improved their lot had they followed the stellar examples of the cow, the cat, or the ever-resourceful cockroach. (Not that I'm stumping for more cockroaches, but I believe in giving credit where credit is due.)

And to make another point that should be quite obvious to anyone who has been the victim of mean-spirited name calling, how would you like it if you were called slow, lesser, a booby, or a politician? These names make it sound like such creatures belong in remedial education classes, and I for one think that is just plain unhelpful. Names should lift one up, not lower one's self-esteem to the point that a whole species is shamed and either loses the will to live or the ability to think of anything other than itself. We're faster, greater, smarter, and more democratic than that. Re-naming should begin at once, and I believe I have just the way to go about it that should appease all sides of the issue. More on this later, after we've fully addressed the necessity of saving endangered animals in the first place. No point in going all out on this project if the animals aren't worth the effort, or wish to check out for reasons of their own.

Now, one can always argue utility, or benefit, when it comes to discussing the need to save such creatures. I get that. I have a nephew whose own parents even call good for nothing, and frankly we're all on the verge of just cutting him loose and leaving him to deal with the fates on his own. I would argue though that even if the purpose of his existence is only to serve as a warning to others, that still counts as a benefit. I'm not going to go ranking these things. I think that would invite trouble.

Besides, there's much we don't understand about creatures like the glass lizard or the crocodile bird or the proboscis monkey, to name but a few more. They may all have a utility that has simply not yet been discovered, though if they keep on with this disappearing kick they've been on lately, we may never know. On second thought, I would be OK with crossing the crocodile bird off of any list aimed at saving it. I believe they would keep right on with their reckless behavior of flying into crocodile's mouths no matter how much they were advised against it.

So now that we're all agreed on the need to save endangered animals, we just need to find a way to do it, more than ever now that the endangered species protection law has itself been placed on life support. Sure we could round up all these creatures and stick them on farms or in zoos or something, and so maybe give them a chance at a meaningful life. It may yet work for my nephew, but on the whole, I think there are likely far too many of these species for that plan to be feasible. I hear there's practically a rush to get on that endangered list. Go figure. I'd like to know what they thought they were signing up for.

No, if we're serious about saving these animals, we'll need lots of resources. Deep pockets. What we need is corporate sponsorship. Now before you call me crazy and stop reading, please hear me out. It's worked in the past for sports and entertainment arenas and events, saving them from extinction time and again. And what have animals been throughout history if not sport and entertainment? Whether we hunt them, watch them, or keep them in cages or aquariums, they are big business. And who knows business better than our corporate leaders. It's time for a truce, and a merging of mutually beneficial interests. And it has precedent. Corporate sponsorship appears to be what has been keeping many politicians afloat.

The only issue I can think of here is that if we invite corporations to have such a business relationship with our endangered animals, we'll likely have to give them re-naming rights. The same arrangement that was made with the owners of the sports and entertainment venues. But as I said before, this can only be an improvement for the morale of many of these animals, and it may even make them feel like a part of something much greater.

Bottom line is I see a win-win here. If a species flourishes with such support, the public will see a corporation that really cares, which is sure to stimulate investment in the corporation. This will lead the corporation to want to do still more for its adoptive species and round and round we go. Who wouldn't travel to see a Nike's Noble Numbat, and think of Nike the next time they were looking for some footwear? Same with the Goldman-Sach's Grand Gharial? The Intel's Imperial Indian Palm Squirrel? The SYSCO's Splendid Sea Squirt? The business possibilities are endless, and currently growing as fast as the endangered list.

Support big business and save the animals!

CEILINGS ARE NOT LIMITATIONS

It occurred to me the other day when things were occurring to me at an unusual clip, that ceilings are important. I don't mean important in the prosaic, roof over your head kind of way, or even in the way that floors are important. Believe me, I know that floors are important. I'm not trying to undervalue them in the least. But you know as well as I do they are rather dull. They just don't inspire one in the same way a ceiling does. Floors do not make you wonder what's beyond them. We all know the answer to that. It's dirt. Always dirt.

Ceilings, on the other hand, have always had to deal with an undeserved rap. But the way I see it, they are not limitations as is commonly believed. They are mysteries filled with possibilities. One does not know what lies beyond them. It could be anything. And who has not stared at a common, blank ceiling and seen fantastic scenes played out before one's eyes, or abstract color saturated designs swirling and pulsing with energy and life. I hope it's not just me.

Architects, not the box builders but those design masters imbued with the spirit and passion of the Ultimate Design Master, have understood these things forever. In order to reach God, or at least to get as close as we can humanly get, we must look up. We must rise above our earthly constraints, above the smoke and mirrors of our daily lives and into the clear, crisp air of possibility. These masters know that to have the possibility of reaching God, you must ADD ceilings, not eliminate them. The Dubai Tower for example, the Burj Khalifa, the tallest building in the world, is over one hundred sixty ceilings high, each one a mystery on the ladder to God. To look from the topmost rung is to look across His Holy Kingdom, and feel overwhelmed by the mystery of the empty desert wasteland that reaches as far as the eye can see.

Of course Michelangelo also saw nothing but possibilities when he painted his masterpiece, the ceiling of the Sistine Chapel. It took him four years to paint it, four long years of looking up at that ceiling with his neck bent and his eyes raised heavenward, four painfully long years of glorifying God with every brush stroke. It was immediately hailed as a work of genius. Viewers were brought to tears, swept away by the holiness of the ceiling visions.

It was a different story for Michelangelo, however. Afterwards he nearly went blind. After four years spent with his head at such an unnatural angle, his eyes only looking up, it would be many years before his sight returned to normal. The threat of losing his sight scared him so badly that for the rest of his life he would struggle to understand the possibility of glorifying God while still managing to see straight.

I'll say it again, ceilings are not limitations, they are possibilities. Unless, of course, they are made out of glass. In which case they will shatter like the possibilities of a businesswoman in a Fortune 500 company.

ISAAC NEWTON

When Isaac Newton tried to grapple,
With the reason for an apple
Falling down upon his head,
He didn't just get mad, instead ...

He quickly started on a mission,
Of scientific repetition.
So gravity was not discovered,
Until poor Isaac had recovered..

ROBERT OPPENHEIMER

It didn't really please his mom,
When Robert made the atom bomb.
"How could you, Robert?" she exclaimed.
"Don't you feel the least ashamed?"

"Atom bombs," he said, "don't kill,
It's people using them who will."
She countered, "Well then make some bread,
And let them drop your loaves instead."

SIGMUND FREUD

"A dream," said Freud, "can set you free,
Psychoanalytically.
Exposing truths within your mind,
That your conscience just can't find.

But still my own dreams puzzle me,
Cause since I made this theory
I can't figure what it means,
To dream about a hill of beans."

PHILO T. FARNSWORTH

Mr. Farnsworth, Philo T.,
Designed and built our first T.V.
Moving images through air,
Invisibly, from here to there.

"That was easy," forewarned he,
"Next to the future of T.V.
It will be harder, I can vouch,
Moving people off the couch."

FLOORS
IT DOESN'T GET
ANY LOWER

So I've recently received an angry response to an earlier essay I wrote about ceilings, accusing me in no uncertain terms of making false comparisons on the general worthiness and respectability of floors, vis a vis ceilings. In brief, it claimed that I had given short shrift to floors because of an unjust bias, and was signed 'Floored in Albuquerque'.

Let me respond:

First of all, Al, (now please don't get all uppity again, Albuquerque is simply too unwieldy to keep repeating), I hope you are speaking as a private citizen and not as a member of the Floor Lobby. Or the Lobby Floor for that matter. I meant no disrespect. Just because I praised ceilings doesn't mean I have it out for floors. I don't, and my aim in writing this response is to prove it to you, and to satisfy all parties similarly concerned. I fully intend to rectify this situation here and now and clarify exactly where I stand on floors, just as soon as I figure out what shrift is. (You leave me at a bit of a disadvantage here, Al, as your letter fails to clarify this, and further fails to identify what you believe an appropriate level of shrift to be.)

Al, most people know me as a generous person. When I decide to give something, I give unreservedly, and the recipients are appreciative. You must excuse my awkwardness, Al, but I'm not used to receiving complaints about my philanthropy. I'm trying to be understanding here, but the fact is that the more I think about the situation you've put me in, the angrier I get. Who the hell are you, Al, to go around accusing me of giving insufficient shrift? That's just not me. I think it highly likely that any shrift I gave would have been more than satisfactory. And never a word of thanks. But did you hear me complain?

On second thought, Al, I think you are either a damned liar, or you're trying to pull a fast one. I don't know how I could have given any shrift at all to floors, of any amount, if I don't know what the hell it is. Do you actually think that I go around giving things without knowing what I'm doing? Just what do you take me for? If you think you're gonna wheedle some shrift out of me in this manner, you are sadly mistaken. I wasn't born yesterday, Al. So take your shrift and shove it!

P.S. If floors got any shrift from me at all, it was purely accidental, and I want it back.

THE GREAT VIKING MAKEOVER

I am a Viking. I learned this recently when I read that anyone of Scandinavian descent whose name ends in 'son' is likely to have Viking blood in their veins. I know it's probably not very Viking-like of me, but I have been afraid of admitting this possibility to myself forever. I only felt emboldened to accept my heritage because of recent scientific discoveries that put Vikings in a better light. And let's face it, a total eclipse of the sun would have put Vikings in a better light.

I am not a practicing Viking mind you. I never have, and likely never will go around raiding, burning, pillaging, wearing horned helmets, drinking from human skulls, and just generally going berserk. But who didn't do these things back in the carefree Viking days of the 9th, 10th, and 11th centuries?

Well, in the Great Viking Makeover, it turns out that laying waste to the non-Viking world was only a part time job, and they never did wear horned helmets or drink from skulls. And only a small percentage of them were genuine berserkers, ingesting psychotropic plants like henbane or fly agaric to put themselves into a trance-like rage, howling and biting their shields while wearing wolf or bear skins into battle. But I think that every group has a few people like that, don't they? We've just learned to look the other way.

In fact, Vikings didn't have a lot of time for marauding shenanigans, thanks in part to those long, cold northern winters. Sure, they made the most of the time they had, terrorizing and ransacking their way through Europe and Russia from innovatively designed longboats that took them far up rivers to places the more run-of-the-mill raiders couldn't go. But in my mind at least, that was just an early demonstration of what has widely come to be regarded as Scandinavian efficiency. I will admit that Scandinavian efficiency is probably much more appreciated now-a-days.

Most of the time Vikings were too busy farming, fishing, building boats, and exploring. It is unfortunate that they are not remembered more for their farming and fishing prowess, but then who is? Viking boat builders however were known to be far ahead of their time, and their ships took fearless explorers on expeditions deep into Russia, southern Europe, and the Middle East, and west to Iceland and Greenland. As there wasn't yet anything to pillage in Iceland or Greenland, they continued west and even reached North America well before it became a popular marauding destination.

The Great Viking Makeover has also turned up evidence that Vikings liked to play games as much as anyone, and tell stories and poems to cheer their hearts during the long winter nights. One popular game had players split into two teams, with each trying to prove which could drink the most mead while delivering the most cutting insults. This usually led to another game in which all Vikings excelled – sword play – which featured a very different type of cutting insult. Stories and poems were told by the winners of these games, and they were no slackards when it came to word play either. Many Viking words greatly enlivened these sagas and are still in use today, such as slaughter, ransack, berserk, knife, club, hit, and skull.

And strangely enough, the new discoveries also reveal that any self-respecting Viking worth his name even bathed once a week, and in hot springs, not the blood of his victims. That's saying something when Vikings tended to have names like Eric Bloodaxe, Thorir the Troll-Burster, and Harald War Tooth. Not only that, hip Vikings usually wore eyeliner, dyed their hair blond if it wasn't already, and had it styled in fabulous braids. Perhaps not so strangely, no one criticized them.

Lastly, Viking society was also far ahead of its time in regard to women's rights. Viking women could own property, hold jobs outside the home, get a divorce, and be a warrior if they so wanted. They did not, as previously believed, merely stay at home and scold their men when they came back late from a raiding party.

I am a Viking, and am now proud to admit it. Perhaps there is hope for all you Huns, Vandals, and Visigoths yet.

HOW SMART ARE SQUIRRELS?

"Squirrels are extremely intelligent creatures." I came across this statement in an article I read that was intended to educate readers with some facts about squirrels. Now, I know there are writers out there who like to play fast and loose with facts, but it makes me shudder to think of a world where people would go about their lives believing this to be true. To be fair, I'm sure the odds alone would have it that some squirrels are fairly bright, at least by squirrel standards. But I have to wonder if the unidentified writer wasn't operating under the same standards.

I think my umbrage at this issue is entirely warranted. The writer's sole reason in making this statement is based on the fact that squirrels, if they notice birds or other squirrels watching them, will pretend to hide food in one place before stashing it in another. In other words, they are masters of deception. I suppose if you are inclined to think that lying is the apotheosis of intelligence, you might fall for this. You would only be deceiving yourself, and what would that say about your intelligence? No, I have the uneasy feeling that even as I write this, the writer is busy hiding even more squirrelly "facts" elsewhere.

Naturally, my suspicions first fell on The Squirrel Lover's Club, whose members believe that whether one is for or against squirrels, squirrels matter. Far be it from me to suggest that squirrels don't matter, though I would hope that with the way squirrels routinely challenge cars, and in the cars own habitat no less, the SLC has noticed that squirrels don't seem to matter much even to themselves, for I have yet to see a squirrel win. Still, with their charming newsletter, "In a Nutshell," and their establishment of the October Squirrel Awareness and Appreciation Month, I suspect the SLC to be more about the fun loving side of squirrels. As to the intelligence side, I have not yet seen any evidence of it in either squirrels or the SLC.

Rodentologists might also find it in their interest to hype the squirrel because of the other more unseemly rodents they study - moles, rats, mole-rats, and pocket gophers, to name a few. (I don't know about you, but the thought of pocket gophers makes me want to quit wearing pants. I think it would be less humiliating.) In case it helps, rodentologists are mammologists who lack the self-respect that comes from studying our more respectable animals. They might have an uphill slog, but they are still as dedicated to the truth as the rest of the mammologists.

A rodentologist is more likely to note that there are 285 species of squirrels; that they can be found on every habitable continent except Australia; and that there are three varieties – tree squirrel, ground squirrel, and flying squirrel. They have not said what squirrels have against Australia, or why the flying squirrels at least have not checked it out. Perhaps it's why they leave the intelligence question alone, instead settling for calling squirrels clever. Now from my experience, calling something, or someone, clever, is what people do when they don't expect much from them, but for personal reasons I don't want to get into that right now.

Rodentologists have also observed that squirrels have four toes on their front feet, and five on their back feet. When asked why, they don't have an intelligent response, or even a clever one. You didn't expect one, did you? They also have noted that squirrels are omnivores, and besides nuts and seeds, will eat plants, insects, and small animals. Your cat should be safe, though if you ever see the three foot giant Malabar purple squirrel, all bets are off.

Squirrels are extremely athletic creatures. That is an actual statement of fact, as demonstrated by their ability to leap 20 feet; run 20 mph; fall 90 feet without getting hurt; glide up to 160 feet if they're of the flying variety; and turn their ankles 180 degrees when running quickly up and down trees. As we all know, however, athleticism and intelligence aren't necessarily a matched pair. Regarding squirrels, just ask any motorist.

Squirrels are one of the primary causes of power outages across the U.S., typically a result of their tendency to either chew through electrical insulation, or contact two conductors of different electrical potentials. This doesn't do much for the squirrels either. Squirrels are also one of the primary choices as the main course for a wide variety of predators. Neither of these facts do much to further the writer's claim of squirrel intelligence.

Psychologists tell us that a rough estimate of intelligence is provided by the brain to body weight ratio.

Squirrels, with a brain the size of a walnut, have a ratio of 0.67, compared to the average human ratio of 2.0. To put this into language that both humans and squirrels can understand, this is nuts, as it means that the average human is only three times smarter than a squirrel. I don't think I'd be the first to suggest that squirrels may be smarter than psychologists, who have never been considered average humans anyway, but that's about as far as I'm willing to go. In any case, I can finally deduce that a psychologist would have been the likely culprit to declare squirrels extremely intelligent. Either that or one of our brighter squirrels.

CLOUDY WITH A CHANCE OF DAYDREAMS

Growing up, my parents would tell me that I could move mountains if I worked hard and dreamed big. To this day I don't know if they were hoping for a business leader or an explosives expert. Either way, that was before I ever saw a mountain. To my parents everlasting disappointment I soon settled for moving clouds. I found them much more cooperative subjects. (I believe this was when my parents changed tactics, and settled for trying to move me out of the house.)

If you move a mountain, what have you accomplished? The mountain is still there, it's just in a different location, and likely in someone else's way now. And for your efforts, you will undoubtedly find yet another mountain in your way also. But if you move a cloud, you will have the whole universe in front of you.

I have been a cloud watcher ever since I realized the limitations of staring at ceilings. The sky spoke to me early on, and while it didn't yet make any more sense than anything on earth, at least it wasn't trying to fill my head with things like algebra, world wars, and "Great Expectations". But while the sky is interesting in its own infinitely mysterious way, it would be a whole lot less interesting without clouds. Clouds bring the sky's magic down to earth, so to speak, in a free show that anyone can appreciate. Even if your imagination is for mature audiences only. No one has to know.

To lay on a grassy lawn on a warm summer day and conduct a parade of cumulous floats slowly across the sky is far more satisfying to me than moving mountains. And I don't have to lift a finger to do it. I am no nephologist however. Nephologists are cloud scientists, people whose business it is to demystify clouds with scientific explanations. They might just as well de-mistify them while they're at it, for clouds with either their magic or their water removed cease to be clouds in my mind. Of course, my mind is always in at least a partly cloudy condition, so I may be biased.

Instead, I'll throw my lot in with the CAS, the Cloud Appreciation Society, a loose affiliation of cloud lovers whose business it is to fight 'blue-sky thinking' wherever they find it. It is a battle that only those with their heads in the clouds would consider, as the blue-sky thinkers have managed to convince most people that 'being under a cloud' is a bad thing. The CAS has countered with a phrase of their own, 'A Day with Your Head in the Clouds Keeps Your Feet on the Ground', but blue-sky thinkers just smile and point to the dark clouds on the CAS horizon.

Word has it that its illustrious founder, Gavin Pretor-Pinney, is finding running the CAS too much work, a concept guaranteed to set its 50,000 members running faster than a sky filled with cumulo-nimbus thunderheads. As author of "The Cloud Spotter's Guide," Pretor-Pinney has no doubt seen the dark clouds as well. It didn't help when he decided to take on the formidable World Meteorological Organization on his own. As publisher of "The International Cloud Atlas," the WMO, established in 1950, recognizes 10 genera of clouds, 14 species, 9 varieties, and dozens of 'accessory clouds' and 'supplemental features'. It does not recognize either sheep or fluffy bunnies.

Pretor-Pinney, however, recognized in 2009 that the WMO had missed one, a rare, wave-like cloud variety that he called 'Asperatus'. In what should be no surprise to anyone, the WMO forecast team never saw either the cloud or the storm that followed. But after eight long years of fighting Pretor-Pinney, they finally caved in 2017 and amended the Atlas, while ungraciously changing the name to 'Asperitus'. Still, it's proof enough to me that sometimes you can move mountains simply by watching clouds.

To my mind, Pretor-Pinney may have had an advantage that the meteorologists didn't have. Cloud watchers are nothing if not contemplative dreamers, and clouds an ever-changing Rorschach test for their souls. Whether you see fluffy bunnies, fierce dragons, or a mushroom cloud surrounded by angels praying, there is much they can tell you about yourself. With so much free psychotherapy, that other elusive cloud, Cloud 9, is always within their grasp. Stick that in your bleeping Atlas, WMO.

BRAIN POWER

Did you know that our brains produce electricity? Of course you did. I'm guessing that like most school kids in science class you stuck electrodes in a dead frog or a potato and seen the voltmeter jump. Am I right? Then later on you may have seen The Matrix and worried about a future where humans are exploited as living batteries. The Matrix was science fiction of course, but it's not such a leap from dead frogs and potatoes to the human brain. I'm quite sure our brains can do anything they can. But I bet you don't know how much electricity our brains generate.

Well let me just say that you can forget those grand dreams of tapping into your brain and powering up your car, your computer, or even your hair dryer. It turns out that our huge 3-pound brains, the pride of the animal kingdom, only produce enough electricity to power a dim light bulb. That's only marginally better than a potato or a dead frog. Talk about a letdown.

But being a glass half full kind of a guy, I quickly began to see the positive side of this. First of all, we're already accustomed to lugging a 3-pound brain around, and

I don't think any of us would consider trading it for a potato or a dead frog just to be able to generate a bit of light to look for our dropped keys in the dark. Besides, I started to thinking that if we got to powering light bulbs or other low wattage appliances with our brains, it would undoubtedly siphon off some or all of the juice our brains need for everyday brain functions. And where would that leave us? No better than a potato or a dead frog, I'm thinking. I would probably never even had that thought if my brain power was otherwise utilized.

So I guess what I'm saying is that while I'm disappointed in my brain's potential as a power source, I needn't be concerned anymore about it's being exploited as a living battery. And nuts to all those people who tell me that I shouldn't worry about it's being exploited as a thinking source either. Dim bulbs, all of them.

THE PATH

One sought inner wisdom,
The other outer truth.
Both of them were travelers.
Each of them a sleuth.

Their paths though intersected,
Where illusion meets with lies,
So they figured truth and wisdom
Must be wearing a disguise.

So back again they travelled,
And unmasked every delusion,
But their paths met yet again,
At the start of their confusion.

DON'T WAIT UP

"Infinity, Infinity,
Forever I will wait for thee.
I miss you so. Please come back home.
Yours in time, Eternity."

"Wait all you want, Eternity.
Forever I must flee from thee.
Further, further, I must roam.
Lost in space, Infinity."

CAT RESEARCH FOR DUMMIES

The hardest working animal researchers in the business have to be the cat researchers. If you don't believe me, try getting a grant to study cats. The grant people will gladly give you all you need to study the mating behavior of the semipalmated sandpiper, or the social life of coral gobies, but give them a whiff of a study you're proposing to find out whether humans domesticated cats or cats domesticated humans, and they'll stare at you like you've got cat scratch fever. Such proposals are destined to end up in the litter box more often than a cat with parasites.

One of the earliest attempts to find out what, if anything, is in a cat's head didn't occur until 2005, when a naïve cognitive researcher conducted the pointing test on cats. This test, for those who might need it pointed out to them, was conceived to determine if a cat could understand where a person is pointing. The first sign the researcher was naïve was when he called it the pointing test, instead of something like the Directional Focus and Awareness Assessment as any seasoned researcher would have done.

The second sign occurred when most cats promptly walked away from the test, thereby pointing more than anything to the need for more testing of cat researchers. It was ten years before anyone sufficiently clueless was found to try again. Cats, in the meantime, continued their research on humans. No grants were needed, as there was no shortage of eager participants willing to work for an occasional purr.

It's no secret that cat researchers have always been envious of dog researchers, mainly because dogs evolved from a social and cooperative animal, the gray wolf. After 30,000 years of habitation with humans, and 9,000 years of selective breeding, dogs have learned to recognize emotion in humans, understand some human speech, and perform socially complex tasks.

By contrast, cats evolved from the Near Eastern wildcat, an antisocial loner who needs 19 square miles of territory for itself or it starts to feel like the world's becoming too crowded. Still, after only 10,000 years of living with humans and 1,000 years of selective breeding, cats have learned how to get humans to feed them, clean their litter box, pet them at times of their choosing, and, if 19 square miles aren't available, to otherwise leave them the hell alone. They likely look at dogs as needy, bootlicking fools, and are quite prepared to wait 20,000 years if necessary before evolving any further.

In later cognitive testing attempts, cats scratched, bit, hid under furniture, leapt out of mazes, and if the researchers weren't already up them, climbed trees. "If you want results on one cat," said one frustrated researcher, "you have to test three." I suspect any cooperative cats were summarily shunned by the others, and stripped of their cat independence rights.

Instead of waiting for University researchers to make any headway on cat cognition, there are simple tests you can try with your own cat at home. All you need is patience, tranquilizers, and a pillow to scream into, as cats are sensitive to loud noises. The first test explores whether or not your cat actually likes you, by placing treats and toys near to where you are sitting to see where your cat lingers. If the cat chooses you, it likely means that you didn't follow directions and gave the tranquilizer to the cat instead of yourself.

To test whether your cat is tuned in to your emotions, sit near a frightening new object and talk calmly to it. If your cat remains agitated, it likely means that you have no influence over your cat. Now there's a stretch. If your cat calms down, it likely means that your cat is in fact influenced by your emotions. To punish you for conducting this cruel experiment however, it will then test YOUR emotions by clawing the leather couch, peeing on the new rug, or ignoring you for the rest of the day.

To test whether your cat knows its name, say several random words of similar lengths and accents, pausing between each. Then say your cat's name. If your cat reacts in the slightest to any of the words, you could be on your way to a new career as a cat researcher.

Some final notes: The results of these tests can actually mean anything you want them to mean, as your cat is liable to change its responses the next time you try to understand it. And if you still don't think that cats are smart and manipulate us, then why is the internet awash in cat videos? As smart and social as dogs are, they haven't begun to figure out the value of social media.

HOPE ON THE ROPES

Hope is a small, unremarkable word for a super-sized task. In a given human life it has to go from non-existent at birth to maximum levels just prior to death, and the working conditions under which it lives in the interval are truly horrific. Abusive actually.

Hope, in fact, takes more punishing hits in a lifetime than a lead-footed boxer. It practically lives on smelling salts. Which is probably why it tends to spread itself out more or less evenly across the world. Think of it from hope's perspective. Spread the impact and live to fight another day. The odds of it going down from a punishing hit in everyone at the same time is fairly remote. Were it to happen though, it would likely mean one thing and one thing only – the apocalypse is nigh.

In any case, from time to time hope makes it clear that it does not like to be trifled with. But that's just hope acting tough, trying to hit above its weight, because it cannot, in fact, afford to be trifled with. It has been in concussion protocol far too often, and for far too long, and questions regarding its sanity are only increasing. At times lately it has engaged in shocking displays of cowardice and self-doubt, and appeared ready to throw in the towel. Which may not be as terrible as it sounds. It may in fact indicate that it is finally facing the truth that its foundation is weak, its feet slow and its legs wobbly, and that it will need to adapt if it is to survive. It can be done. The Greatest, Muhammad Ali, successfully did so with his rope-a-dope strategy. If you're going to spend more time on the ropes, you must learn to use them to your advantage, for the dopes are sure to keep coming.

At the very least, if not less, and in defiance of all that is reasonable, hope is resilient. It floats; it bounces back; it soars even. It takes a nine count, picks itself up off the mat, and grins like it never knew what hit it. Which, given all the concussions, is probably true.

CLASSICAL ANATOMY BACH VS BEETHOVEN

A discordant note was heard in the classical music world recently when a German anatomist injected new controversy into the age-old argument as to who was the greater talent, Johann Sebastian Bach, or Ludwig Van Beethoven. The scientist analyzed a photo of a skeleton believed to be that of Bach, and concluded that the 5' 11" pianist/composer had an advantage Beethoven was lacking – enormous hands. He claimed that his giant hands would have allowed him a fantastic reach spanning twelve white keys, an octave and a half, fully a half octave greater than the diminutive Beethoven, who at 5' 2" undoubtedly had trouble even getting up on the piano stool without assistance.

The only response from the Beethoven camp to date has been to say that Bach looked like a donkey and smelled like one too. (It should be noted that this claim has not been verified by any member of the scientific community, although there have been whispers, since it has been notoriously difficult to reconstruct Bach's appearance from his skull.) Concerning Beethoven though, an 1863 analysis of his disinterred skull revealed that it was twice as thick as normal, with prominent cheekbones and forehead. The analysis went on to report that this would have produced a lion-like appearance. Hearing this news, the Bach camp couldn't stop braying.

As we await further news in this ever-widening rift, it got me to wondering what other classical music titans were influenced by their anatomical peculiarities.

The 6' 0" Franz Liszt could go Bach one note better, with hands that were able to span a mind-boggling 13 keys. This incredible feat and his virtuoso playing owed a lot to the fact that, unlike most people, the connective tissue between his fingers appeared absent, actually starting below the base of his fingers. As a result his hands could spread so wide that he likely could have palmed both Bach's and Beethoven's skulls.

Sergei Rachmaninov's hands could also span a 13th, but he was 6' 6" tall. He is also believed to have had Marfan's Syndrome, and show me a syndrome which doesn't help in explaining things.

Frederic Chopin makes for an interesting case study in using one's head to get the most out of one's hands. At only 5' 6" tall, it was said that he had very small hands, but such wide spaces between his fingers that one observer noted that "his hands would suddenly expand like the opening of the mouth of a serpent about to swallow a rabbit whole." It has been reported that he created those wide spaces himself by sleeping with wine corks between his fingers. I'm thinking that this could go a long way in explaining his famous dexterity at the keyboard as well, since keeping supplied with fresh corks would have certainly kept the wine glasses filled.

On hearing of Chopin's corks, Robert Schumann thought he could do better, but he clearly was not the thinker, or drinker, that Chopin was. He was either short, middling, or tall. Probably disappointed in the size of his hands, he first tried tying his little fingers back. When that didn't produce the desired results, he created a mechanical hand stretching device out of a cigar box and wire, which was said to have looked like a medieval torture implement. This was probably around the time that his music took a dark and brooding turn, sounding as if somebody was torturing him. Still not satisfied, he cut the webbing between his fingers, developed sepsis, and died, apparently never hearing, or heeding, the very sage advice Chopin always gave on hand stretching to his students: Drink more wine. (Of course this was the advice he gave on all subjects.)

Finally I give you Franz Schubert, who may have been so despondent over his 5' 0" frame and small hands that he only lived thirty years. It could not have helped that his nickname was 'the little mushroom'. But he did write the deep and mysterious F minor Fantasy. Then again, his hands were so small that he had to write it for four hands instead of two like the big boys.

COLLECTING - A HOBBY FOR PSYCHOANALYSTS

Collectors are a strange lot. We're always on the lookout for that next piece, which makes us both perpetually dissatisfied that our collections aren't complete, but eternally optimistic that we'll get there. This makes our cups, the ones we don't collect, both half empty and half full. But definitely never running over. Unless you're a psychoanalyst who collects collectors.

Psychologists say that everyone collects something. And whether they collect cups, cats, cars, kids (mostly just photographic reproductions, though with some only the originals will do), or rejection notices from publishers, people's passions have stories to tell. (Not that publishers want to hear them. I'm pretty sure they just collect broken dreams, but maybe that's my obsession talking.) While the psychologists would undoubtedly have plenty to say about what your collection of medieval torture devices means, to me, a better story is the one about why we're obsessed to collect things in the first place.

Our earliest ancestors were collectors, and if they hadn't excelled at collecting nuts, berries, and wooly mammoth hides, it would have been the Grim Reaper collecting their genes instead of us. Survival drove these early collectors, not passion, though I for one am thankful that they were at least passionate about survival, if not so much their unvarying diet of nuts and berries. But they had to be cautious, as nuts, berries, and mammoth hides were not yet available for bargain prices at flea markets. It's probably a good thing, as besides fleas, these would have also been prime marketplaces for saber-toothed tigers, who had their own collecting priorities.

Modern collectors don't have to fear saber-toothed tigers of course, but if you've ever arrived at an estate sale for the opening bell, you've no doubt battled plenty of blood thirsty sharks to get that vintage kitchen tin that subconsciously brought control and contentment to your world. That's what many psychologists say anyway, that in a world full of chaos and insecurity, collecting provides an emotional connection to the comfort and security of the nourishing breast. They would say that. I think psychologists would connect any human behavior to the nourishing breast if you let them.

Unless you happen to be consulting a Freudian psychologist. The granddaddy of all psychologists would find a way to tie even psychologists from the nourishing breast camp to unresolved toilet training issues, and that's what they've done to collectors too. And I had always supposed a simple flush resolved any lingering toilet issues. They would have us believe however that this is what children in the anal retentive stage of development actually fear – the loss of their "possessions", and that this is what drives us to collect things to this day. As Freud was a major collector himself, something tells me that his is one collection I would never want to see. It's never too late to give one's unresolved issues a quick flush.

If pressed, however, say beneath a heavy object, most psychologists will admit that collecting is simply an enjoyable activity. It has the excitement of the hunt, the satisfaction of the display, the social camaraderie of bonding with like-minded collectors, and the feelings of superiority or envy that inevitably come when comparing yourself to those like-minded collectors. Even under pressure, the chance to analyze those feelings is like mother's milk to psychologists, and will make them squirm in anticipation. This would be a good time to remind them of their own unresolved issues with either the nourishing breast, their early toilet training, or the pressure they're under to blame all human behavior on such infantile theories.

Whether our collections are museum noteworthy or ball of string insignificant, if everyone collects something we can't all have such unresolved issues, can we? The Government collects taxes. God and the Devil collect souls. If you want to tell them about their unresolved issues, be my guest, but I think it would be more fun to let the psychologists tell them.

THE CONNECTICUT STATE ANIMAL YOU'VE NEVER SEEN

I'm willing to bet that the average reader of this book, as sharp and observant as he or she may be, couldn't both name the Connecticut state animal and claim to have ever seen one. I'll also extend the same bet to all the above and below average readers. Here's a hint: This dubious honor was bestowed upon the animal in 1975 by the state's General Assembly, which, while not being technically incompetent, liked to work at it more than in other years. They thought that a state animal would take people's minds off the high tax rate, and that year it might have worked if they had chosen an animal that everybody could get behind.

This immediately excluded elephants and donkeys, and seemed to improve the odds on snakes and weasels, but politics being what it is, the two sides instead went back and forth with all manner of other animals they thought best represented the Land of Steady Habits. Legislative habits proved steadier however, and eventually all animals became roadkill. So while this General Assembly seemed more underwater than most, yet still unable to tell a crustacean from a cetacean, they naturally compromised on the sperm whale. Although no one had ever seen one, they were all fairly sure that at the very least they wouldn't have to worry about the new state animal ever being squashed on Connecticut's busy roadways. They also may have thought that if they could sell the state on laws that didn't make sense, they could do the same for any animal they chose, even an animal whose sole relationship with Connecticut came at the business end of a harpoon. As it was with Moby Dick and Captain Ahab's ship, The Pequod, some say it was the sperm whale that sank the 1975 Connecticut General Assembly.

Some facts about Connecticut's state animal:

- A sperm whale has the largest brain of any creature that ever existed, larger even than the combined brains of the 1975 General Assembly.
- Sperm whales can reach 65 feet in length, which means that 812 of them laid end to end would stretch from Old Saybrook, CT to East Marion, NY, the former proposed site of a bridge spanning Long Island Sound. This information is offered for reference purposes only, not as a design suggestion.
- They can dive over 4,000 feet in search of their favorite prey, giant squid and cuttlefish.
- Sperm whales have never been seen in Connecticut waters, possibly owing to Long Island Sound only having an average depth of 63 feet. Diving in such waters when you're 65 feet long is not advisable.

Additionally, Long Island Sound is totally lacking in giant squid and cuttlefish.
- Sperm whales are the largest of the toothed whales. Their 40 – 50 teeth each weigh over two pounds. Either despite this or because of this, they rarely chew their food. It should be noted that toothless whales do not chew their food either. Chewing never seemed to catch on as a whale behavior somehow.
- They are called sperm whales because of a waxy substance found in their heads called spermaceti, which was formerly used to make candles and ointments. They have never gotten over this.
- A sperm whale has a huge head, which takes up nearly a third of its body length. And this was before being named Connecticut's state animal.
- They live 50 – 70 years and generally die of natural causes, unless a whaling ship finds one first. They are considered endangered, when they are considered at all.
- Sperm whales make the loudest sound of any animal on earth. Divers have described it as sounding remarkably like "HELP!"

SEASHELLS

Did you know that all those seashells
That you see on every shore,
Were once houses for some creatures
Crawling on the ocean floor?

Now imagine walking on the beach,
With seashells in your sack,
When all those homeless creatures
Come to take their houses back.

THE BIG TRICK

Before the Big Bang there was nothing at all,
And after, a whole universe,
Of planets and stars and space and time,
As immense as it is diverse.

Like pulling doves from a bottomless hat,
That magician's trick is a riot,
But if he can do it with the Big Bang,
He can undo it with the Big Quiet.

THE TROUBLE WITH AMOEBAS

If huge amoebas ruled the world,
We'd be in lots of trouble.

By zillions they'd outnumber us,
And that's before they double.

Amorphous blobs that will absorb us
Till we all succumb,

Unless they're eaten first
By giant paramecium.

SELFISH TO THE END

As the Doomsday Clock ticks relentlessly on, I can't help but think what it's doing to my social life. So call me selfish. I know that I'm not doing enough about it. To be perfectly honest, I guess I'd have to say that I'm not really doing anything about it. Except to read. Which is how I came across a fascinating article in The End Times entitled, 'Apocalypses – You Can't Live With Them And You Can't Live Without Them'.

I have to say that the article hit a nerve, and made me more fearful than ever. But at least it justified my lack of action. You may or may not feel the same. I'll reprint it here and let you decide what to do about the end of the world:

"Selfishness evolved as the default moral code in humans, and beats altruism hands down. The strongest survival instincts are selfish ones, the ones that let us hit that squirrel instead of swerving recklessly into a tree. Or buy a bigger car or house than we need instead of helping others out of homeless shelters. That's what guilty feelings are for. Fortunately, guilt is among the weakest feelings, and can easily be avoided if one simply thinks of squirrels as furry rats, or avoids getting anywhere near homeless people.

But make no mistake, the poor want to be middle class, the middle class want to be rich, the rich want to be super-rich, and for reasons no one has ever understood, the super-rich want still more. Even the Jainist casts an envious eye on the Buddhist's luxurious asceticism. It probably has something to do with sex, like pretty much everything else. Go ask the immeasurably rich sheikhs with their harems the size of amusement parks.

And although we are very good at turning a blind eye on all this selfishness, all this wanting, wanting, wanting, deep down in the hard to locate rational core of our brains we know that the result of all this greed is the depletion of the vital resources we know to be limited, the trashing of the air, water, land, and biodiversity needed for our survival, the fostering of wars that take us ever closer to oblivion, and the belief in a God to justify it all. In short, apocalypse. Unfortunately, we also know that it is still our best chance. Because if altruism had evolved as the winning moral code, if self-sacrifice was the norm, humans would have left this planet to the furry rats long ago and run head on into the first trees they encountered."

FOOD FIGHT AT THE BIRD FEEDER

How closely do you watch your bird feeder? For the casual observer, likely not close enough to realize that a feathered version of the Hunger Games is taking place right outside your window. Not unlike a cocktail party when the shrimp platter comes out, there's nothing like free food to show how different birds sneak, bluff, threaten, or outright bully their way to the table. But with so many possible bird interactions, the pecking order can be complicated to figure out. (By the way, the term "pecking order" was coined in 1921 by Norwegian psychologist Thorleif Schjelderup-Ebbe, while observing what he realized was a dominance hierarchy in barnyard chickens. Apparently some chickens are more chicken than others.)

Eliot Miller, a researcher at the Cornell Lab of Ornithology, has been closely studying bird feeder power struggles, and with the help of 20,000 backyard bird watchers in his Project Feeder Watch, has been able to sort out the pecking order of 136 common American species. If you're quiet, you might be able to catch Eliot as he shows off his dazzling study to establish himself as the dominant researcher in the lab and attract female ornithologists. In the meantime, thanks to Eliot, we can all watch our feeders with a new fight club-like interest, and a greater appreciation for grocery stores.

Generally speaking, the bigger the bird, the bigger the bully, though there are plenty of birds that punch above their weight. Test your observational skills with these featherweight matchups.

Black-capped chickadee vs. American goldfinch: Despite their flashy feathered finery and a slight size advantage, the goldfinch is more about glam than glory. In fact, it will fly aside to just about every bird at the feeder. Not that the chickadee is such a heavy hitter. It loses out to the tufted titmouse, the white-breasted nuthatch, and even the ground feeding dark-eyed junco. In fact, when the goldfinch isn't around, the chickadee can often be heard complaining about the unfairness of life. No one listens.

European starling vs. Blue jay: An intriguing card with two heavyweight bullies, this matchup is seen by the ornithology oddsmakers as a draw. The blue jay has the bulk, but the starling brings new moves learned from its years battling European birds. With their bullying tactics and messy habits, it's apparent that both enjoy being the bad birds watchers love to hate, but the patriotic choice here would be the American blue jay.

Cardinal vs. Mourning dove: The dove might be the messenger of peace and all, but don't let that fool you. At least not too much. Although usually seen on the ground hunting after food spilled by more aggressive birds, it will still use its bulk to muscle out everybody's favorite, the cardinal. It might be the reason why hunters shoot millions of them every year. Or else they just never got the dove's message.

Red-bellied woodpeckers vs. Red-headed woodpeckers: Heads has it. Although the red-headed woodpecker is a Connecticut endangered species, it still beats out its red-bellied cousin. Interestingly though, starlings beat red-headed woodpeckers, while the red-bellies beat starlings. Who knew bird watching could be like a game of rock-paper-scissors?

Common raven vs. American crow: Both of these titans of the feeder will scare away any other bird, except for a raptor or a turkey. (Some raptors, like the sharp-shinned hawks and Cooper's hawks, look at feeders as buffet tables. For birds, not seed.) Though the raven is much larger than the crow, a group of crows is called a murder. Enough said.

Almost as much fun as watching bird feeder dynamics is watching the different bird watchers in action themselves. When you see a bevy of birdwatchers, the dominant one can always be identified by its billed cap, the very expensive binoculars hanging from its neck, and its habit of pointing at birds no one else can see. Its repetitive hushed call of "There, a loggerhead shrike!" or "There, an Eastern wood-pewee!" can get old fast. The lesser birdwatcher is best differentiated from the dominant by its desperate call of "Where? Where?"

By far the most common bird watcher is the window watcher. This shy but sensitive creature is known for putting out seed for birds and simply sitting by a window to watch them eat it. No one really knows why. It's occasional alarm cry of "#!!*! Squirrel!" has been known to startle nearby persons.

FISHBOWL FANTASIES

Some people have wondered where I stand on the subject of pet fish. Let's be clear about this. Fish are not pets, particularly any you might ever consider baking, broiling, frying, or flushing, and I think that about covers the lot of them. By my definition, a pet must meet just two criteria. First, it must offer some sort of companionship. Second, it must be aware of its owner's omnipotence, and act accordingly. One might be excused for thinking that the second criteria leaves out cats, but shake a container of treats and see who doesn't come running and rubbing itself shamelessly on your legs.

Fish fail miserably on both counts. They are constitutionally incapable of showing the proper deference to the owner who has given them a chance to live in a small bowl, who feeds them tiny flakes of a mysterious yet nutritious substance they would never get to eat in the wild, and who even provides fun décor for their new homes like plastic plants, sunken treasure chests, and statues of Neptune.

And given the glass walls and the few gallons of water between us and them, one could expect more companionship from a tarantula. Unless one was the type that sought out their company on bath night, in which case the ASPCA and the American Psychiatric Association might have something to say about it. Fish are more akin to paintings, in that you look at them without interaction, and nobody has questioned whether paintings are pets. Personally, I have more interaction with my annual wildlife calendar than I could ever have with fish.

Let's face it, fish are novelty items, like lava lamps and modern popular music, which fact is reflected both in their cost to the consumer and their disposability. They are typically sold in a plastic bag for less money than a fish sandwich, which to my mind is the more appropriate way to appreciate fish. I realize that there are some fish that might actually cost more than sushi at a Tokyo restaurant, but that is because of the scarcity of those fish in the wild. Their ownership is simply due to rich or selfish people wanting to own something because of its rarity, and is one of the causes of animal extinctions. Those people should be placed in a fishbowl themselves. See how they like it.

Here is all the evidence you need to show that fish don't meet the criteria to be a pet. They don't develop separation anxiety or destructive behaviors when you leave home. They don't demonstrate the slightest bit of awareness of your being there or not being there. If they knocked over a plastic plant or nibbled the diver's air hose you could at least tell they were upset about something, but all you ever find when you return home are either some oblivious swimming fish or even more oblivious floating fish.

It's true that fish will never upset the neighbors with their barking. In fact I don't believe they make any sound, a characteristic that I find, well, fishy. They'll also never leave a surprise for you on the new rug; need to be walked or cleaned; shed or drool; or track mud or kitty litter all over the house. Instead they are most known for having a tranquil effect on anyone watching them. I would suggest though that anyone wanting to watch them for more than three minutes is already about as tranquilized as one can get without hospitalization, and is probably either in need of a real pet or defibrillation.

BRAIN FARTS
THE BLAME GAME

Generally speaking, the brain is a complicated assemblage of physical, chemical, and electrical parts and properties. I say generally because, well, you never know about some people. To further their goal of understanding the brain and its employers/victims, neuroscientists break it up into smaller units called hemispheres, lobes, ventricles, and areas, with leftover parts that are given names like the thalamus, the hypothalamus, and various other thalamuses.

One of their goals in doing this was quite possibly to search for which section to blame for brain farts, those embarrassing mental lapses that can make even a neuroscientist mistake the cerebrum for the cerebellum. Eventually they were successful and managed to pin the blame on the DMN, and no, the D does not stand for Dog. This is not completely fair because the DMN, or default mode network, is actually a collection of brain regions, which smells suspiciously like it's the result of an evolutionary effort by each section to dodge the blame.

So what actually happens when you suddenly forget your spouse's name, or that your eyeglasses are on top of your head? To put it in plain English, maladaptive brain activity changes occur when the default mode network is activated because of the occurrence of a context shift in the attention network. So now you know. In other words (and thank God for other words), brain farts occur because the brain shifts from Drive into Cruise Control to save energy, and then Bigfoot suddenly runs across the road and causes you to completely forget what you're supposed to be getting at the grocery store.

Not counting Bigfoot sightings, researchers say there are ten common context shifts that are the cause of most brain farts. So put your brain back into Drive and see how many you can blame for past maladaptive brain activity changes.

Probably the most common context shift occurs when you walk through a doorway. Psychologists at Notre Dame have discovered that this triggers an "event boundary" in the mind, which tends to leave thoughts and memories in one room while it prepares a blank slate for the new room. (Don't be too hard on your brain, it can only do so much. Thankfully most houses only have seven or eight rooms, and many brains are already quite blank.)

Shadows are another common trigger, for two reasons. One is because they play tricks on our eyes, and the other is because our minds evolved to understand that they are places where danger lurks. (As danger can lurk in other places as well, I have suggested to the neuroscientists that lurking things in general be elevated to the status of a context shift, but so far have not received a response.

Apparently they have more important things to think about.)

Evolution is also thought to be responsible for the brain farts caused by beeps and photographs. Beeps are an unnatural sound in nature, and our minds still haven't come to grips with them. (Speaking of unnatural sounds, I've heard some farts of the brain-less variety that caused my brain to struggle plenty. My nose too.) The same thing is said to apply when looking at two-dimensional images of people. They are not natural to our evolutionary past. I don't know what this says about all the one-dimensional people running about these days.

In one out of four people, bright lights cause what's known as a "photic sneeze reflex," which blows away any thoughts or memories they were just trying to hold onto. Wide open spaces won't make you sneeze, but they do make you walk in circles. It turns out that wide open spaces are such a jolt to our mind's sense of perspective, that lacking any reference points, it will not only drop everything it was carrying, but make you walk in a loop. Scientists have yet to understand the purpose of the circle walk, though it seems pretty clear that the mind is simply trying to get you back to the point where it lost itself. I believe this is called the circle of life.

Oddly enough, everyone's favorite romantic subject, the moon, has been known to cause less than thoughts of amour, especially when it's low in the sky. At such times it appears much larger than usual, and creates a context shift known as the Ponzo illusion, wherein many a thought has been lost. (I'll leave it between Ponzo and the neuroscientists to make any correlation between love and brain farts.)

The mind is also apparently easily tricked to the point of forgetfulness by something called the "continuous wagon wheel illusion," which is what happens when our minds perceive car wheels as spinning backwards while the car is plainly moving forward. Another thing that gives our brains fits as well as farts is the color red/green. When these colors appear independently, our brains are fine with them. But if our brains should catch them mingling, neurons from warring areas come out firing like the Hatfield's and the McCoy's. There's a reason why we call a red/blue mix purple, but don't have a name for red/green. (It's times like this that I worry about our minds.)

That's nine brain fart inducing context shifts. I know I promised ten, but I just walked through a doorway into a brightly lit room where some infernal device was beeping. I mean, it was the dog.

ARE YOU LOOKING AT ME?

I'm being watched. So are you, most likely. No, I'm not some paranoid conspiracy theorist, I'm a scientist, but it doesn't make any difference. We all see faces in the most unlikely places.

Right now, for instance, an alien lizard queen is staring at me from an oriental rug, complete with flowing robes, tiara, bejeweled necklaces, and incongruously, cat's eye sunglasses. (There's no accounting for taste.) From where I sit I also see a Viking, a clown, Santa Claus, and Thomas the Tank Engine. My whole house in fact is chock full of peculiar apparitions. All staring at me. But I guess as long as they remain two-dimensional and don't talk to me, I'm OK with that. So far, so good, though it does make me feel at times like I'm living in a hidden object puzzle. If I find all the faces, do I win anything?

Our ancient ancestors won big when they solved their hidden object puzzles. They won another day of life, because their hidden faces often came with hidden claws and fangs. We humans, it turns out, evolved with a superpower in solving such puzzles. It's a superpower that was every bit as important as controlling fire, skill with weapons, and the ability to yell "Watch Out!" Being weak, slow, clawless, and fangless, our ancient ancestors would have never gotten off the predator's menu card without these talents.

Scientists today have a name for our face-finding superpower, pareidolia, from the Greek meaning "wrong shape", and blame our brains for misinterpreting what we see. (These are the same types our ancient ancestors would have needed to yell "Watch Out!" to more frequently.) But face the facts, in most of today's world, pareidolia only benefits savvy marketers, religious believers, and of course, daydreamers. It's not likely to save your life, but it can spice it up a bit.

In the market for a new car? Watch Out! The faces on car grilles don't come with claws or fangs, but they are out to get you nonetheless. Masculine, feminine, cute, aggressive, smart looking, happy .... the cars (and their designers and marketers) are calling to you, and they are a great judge of your personality. Somehow they know if you're a cop, a grandmother, or a stamp collector. Stamp collecting grandmotherly cops might throw them however, unless that's who crossover vehicles are for.

Studies have shown that religious believers are more prone to pareidolia than most. From the Shroud of Turin and the Veil of Veronica to the toasted cheese sandwich of Diana Duyser, images of Jesus of Nazareth and the Virgin Mary regularly appear to believers on all sorts of items, many of them edible. Food for the soul, perhaps. Or money in the pocket, depending on one's beliefs. The cheese sandwich sold on eBay for $28,000, leading some to question Ms. Duyser's beliefs, and others to watch what they ate a bit more carefully.

In my opinion though, pareidolia is evolution's vestigial gift to daydreamers, the primary beneficiaries. From the Man in the moon to the alien lizard queen on my rug, strange and curious faces can appear anytime and anywhere to those with their minds set on wander, inviting all sorts of escapist fantasies. They will always be welcome in my house, for they never fail to amuse.

So who's in YOUR house?

WHAT'S THE HURRY?

If the ozone hole don't get us then the global warming will,
And the odds of doing something are approximately nil.
While the scientists are yapping,
All the governments are napping,
And the CEOs are clapping,
STILL,
Who really thinks that climate change can kill?

While there's still a drop of oil left, it's Drill Baby Drill!
Despite the Greenie voices that are sounding rather shrill.
But the money is not lacking,
And with governmental backing,
They will keep on with their fracking,
Still,
What's another pipeline spill?

The forests are all bleeding their green streams of chlorophyll,
All the carbon is escaping and the fauna's looking ill.
But in bungle after bungle,
We're still chopping down the jungle,
Leaving nothing but the fungal,
STILL,
Who cares what really happens in Brazil?

All the congressmen are smiling as they show how well they shill,
For the dirty coal executives with "clean coal" on the bill.
Whether people cry collusion,
Or dig out from their delusion,
Old King Coal needs a transfusion,
Still,
Who needs another blasted hill?

The arctic ice is nearly gone, it's really quite a thrill,
To search the North Pole waters, for old Santa's domicile.
Though the children all seem worried,
That their future will be buried,
Father Christmas won't be hurried,
Still,
What future will the children have to fill?

So throw away your sweaters you'll no longer feel the chill,
And say hello to the ocean from your new home on the hill.
While it may seem like disaster,
We're assured we're still the Master,
And can fix this problem faster,
STILL,
A child has just been born with a gill.

IF KEEPING THE FAITH, TURN DOWN THE TEMPERATURE

Keeping the faith, of course, implies first of all that one has faith to keep. But that is hardly the only demand that faith puts on anyone with half a mind to keep it. That half a mind must also figure out where to keep it so it won't get lost; what to feed it so it won't waver, weaken, or die; and perhaps most critically, be prepared to clean up after it, because not only will it create more unholy messes than you would think possible, but it also loves to roll and thrash in them like a wild beast. It is more difficult than trying to keep a herd of parched elephants from crossing five hundred miles of Kalahari desert in search of a mud wallow. It believes what it wants to believe, despite the lack of evidence to support its existence, and despite the fact that some will lose their way, their will, or the rest of their minds in the relentless blinding light and searing heat of the desert sun.

There are secondary problems as well that are no less daunting. As with all human proclivities, keeping the faith is a transactional one. Are the expectations of the one entering into the transaction reasonable, relative to the levels of risk and effort expended? Take your average aged Grateful Dead fan as an example of one who perhaps keeps an unreasonable amount of faith, collecting concert tapes in the crazed belief that somewhere a tape exists that will transport them to the same places that LSD used to, despite the fact that they all sound like a band taking forever to tune up. Not only are they expending time and money by keeping their faith at levels that are higher than a kite, but it is at the risk of their very minds.

Conversely, the low expectations of a country music fan are much more easily attainable, and one does not have to risk one's mind. As it is about as satisfying as non-alcoholic beer however, faith can be a bit harder to keep. It is a fine balance and one must tread cautiously.

But how long can faith be realistically kept? This is a particularly interesting question, and one that is the subject of much on-going study. Fortunately, faith can be tested. Not under laboratory conditions perhaps, but certainly by applying a wide array of stressors. Stressors like reality, or the devil, for instance. Or the Big Kahuna, one's own mind.

Given these difficulties, it would appear that any faith one is trying to keep would be best kept as close to the heart as possible, before the muckrakers of the mind discover it and send their twisted armies of reason into battle. The heart is like a lockbox, or at least an icebox, and can keep all sorts of perishable items well past their normal expiration date. But it is not inviolable. Double the locks or turn down the temperature if you must, because you do not want to mess with the mind. It is where Doubt awaits, biding its time as it evaluates the hearts defenses.

FERMENTING TROUBLE ANIMALS AND ALCOHOL

For better or worse, the drinking of alcohol is a human custom, possibly dating back to the earliest humans. What with the golden rule of that era being "Eat or be eaten," drinking would have seemed like a good alternative. It should not be surprising then to learn that many other animals also developed an appreciation for this strategy. While humans eventually evolved and developed things like weapons and group counseling, and changed the rule to a much less stressful "Eat and eat some more," other animals did not.

Alcohol consumption never changed in either case, perhaps suggesting that drinking did not correlate with eating after all. In the case of humans however, it did turn out to correlate well with weapons and group counseling. But rather than speculate further on the reasons humans imbibe, let's take a look at some other animal tipplers and see what they have to teach us.

Some birds will literally risk their necks to get wasted. In Vienna, Austria, forty songbirds, who were no doubt singing drinking songs, feasted on fermented berries before flying into buildings and breaking their necks. Similar observations of fruit eating birds have been reported elsewhere, with some birds simply falling out of trees, too drunk to fly. Contrary to rumors, there have been no confirmed reports of these delinquent birds smoking and hanging out at the corner telephone poles.

Bees, ever driven by their communistic subservience to the Hive, know just what to do when anyone comes home drunk on fermented nectar. In their version of group counseling, the impaired bee's peers gang up and prevent it from entering the hive until it proves it can fly in a beeline. But with 60,000 bees per hive, there will always be some who turn to liquid courage to try and find some sense of personal identity.

In a stark contrast from bees, moose are loners, which by itself makes them prime candidates for an alcohol problem. And their enormous size makes the thought of a drunk moose no laughing matter, unless you happen to find one with its antlers caught in a tree. This actually happens in Sweden, where in the autumn, drunk moose getting tangled in trees, swing sets, and Christmas lights are almost as common as fermenting apples. The moose become so inebriated they may believe the trees to be rivals after their apples, or they may be trying to climb the trees to reach some more. The Swedes say moose are funny that way.

I guess you have to give the Malaysian pen-tailed tree shrew credit for trying. All day long it drinks fermented palm nectar, which at 3.8 per cent alcohol should be potent enough to send the rat-sized rodent scurrying for the sewer. Put another way, on any given day if a tree shrew were to get behind the wheel of a car, it would not only be out of its tree, it would also be several times over the legal limit. Yet the shrew never gets drunk. This probably shouldn't surprise us. When was the last time a shrew ever did anything it was expected to?

Like something out of an alcoholic's nightmare, drunk elephant stories abound in Africa and India. In Africa, natives say that elephants get drunk from the fermenting fruit of the Marula tree. Given the size of elephants, and calculations on the amount of fruit they'd need to eat, many scientists dispute this, claiming instead that, "People just seem to want to believe in drunk elephants." Villagers in India believe that scientists wouldn't know a drunk elephant if it trampled them, which is tragically what herds of plastered pachyderms have done to them after bingeing on vats of their rice beer.

This brings us to monkeys, who, from their nearby branch on our evolutionary tree, have been able to watch and learn from the biggest alcohol aficionados of all. On the Caribbean Island of St. Kitts, vervet monkeys, who used to steal fermented sugar cane from the rum industry, are now doing the next best thing to bellying up to the bar – stealing cocktails from tourists. Extensive studies of the drinking habits of these monkeys revealed that most drink in moderation, 12 % drink heavily, and 5 % drink excessively, to the point of stumbling about and starting fights, before vomiting and passing out. Extensive studies on the tourists make the vervet monkeys seem more like Amish teetotalers by comparison.

As the above examples show, many animals have found varied ways to satisfy their alcohol cravings. Why this should be so is another question, and one fraught with many confusing and even contradictory answers. Perhaps Homer Simpson said it best when he said, "Alcohol, the cause of, and solution to, most of life's problems." It doesn't answer the question, but I don't believe either Homer or the other animals are capable of giving us a straight answer.

WALK THIS WAY

Did you ever wonder what your walk says about you? Because your walk talks, and mostly behind your back, to anyone who is paying attention. The Department of Defense is paying attention, going so far as to develop biometric technology that can identify potential terrorists by their walks. While your walk might not get you into trouble, unless you jaywalk, or walk off with the goods, even if you're walking the line it is blabbing plenty about your health, your mood, and even your personality. The only known way to shut it up is to walk off a cliff.

It's no walk in the park if you have bunions, hammertoes, arthritis, or any of the many health problems that affect walking. It's understandable that the varied walking styles of such afflicted people reveal more of their mood than their personality. And nothing sours their mood more than people who tell them to 'Walk it off.' People who say this are walking on thin ice. As for people using canes and walkers to get around, odds are their walks are speaking to a strong desire to be twenty-one again.

Whether you walk on the wild side, sleepwalk, or walk in someone else's shoes, nearly everyone walks. But even if you think you walk to the beat of a different drummer, psychologists say that your walk will likely fall into one of eight styles. (It should be noted that these styles do not include either the competitive walker, who, along with the competitive breather and the competitive sleeper, belongs in a category all their own, or the power walker, who has no style. It is best to walk far around such people if you encounter them.)

If you walk with a slow pace and a relaxed posture, you could be The Chiller. As you might guess, The Chiller is easy going and calm, with an agreeable personality. This is surprising given that a slow pace has also been linked to poorer health, impaired cognition, and a higher risk of death. I believe, however, that The Chiller is smart and chill enough to understand that everyone's life comes with a high risk of death.

The Executive walks at a fast pace with focused strides, and gives off an intense vibe. Beware The Executive, who will walk all over you as if you weren't there. The Executive has a goal-oriented personality, whose goal is to get to the top before you. Don't worry, there's a good chance you will see this person again on the way down. That would be a good time to walk them to the door.

If you see someone walking very slowly with their head down, it's likely because they either lost a lot of money or their best friend. Or perhaps it's just the worry beads they lost a while back. These things indicate that The Worrier has also lost his or her way. The Worrier, who has an introverted and anxious personality, never gets anywhere, and can often be seen walking in circles. This is because they're always worried about the same old things.

The Supporter has smooth, medium-paced, confident strides, and would rather nod and make friendly eye contact than shout or wave. The Supporter is helpful, dependable, a good listener, and will walk into a wall for you if you're on the same team. As you might imagine, this can make it take longer for The Supporter to get anywhere. If you're not on the same team, The Supporter will gladly build a wall for you too.

You will always notice The Showboat walk, arms and hips swaying in an exaggerated, over-confident fashion, with shoulders back and head held high. The Showboat is the Cock of the Walk, and has a very charismatic personality. The Showboat will never be found walking alone, and would probably walk like The Worrier if it came to that.

The Corrector walks hunched over with arms close to the sides, taking small steps, and has the appearance of one walking on eggshells. Such a person has a cautious personality, and is afraid to walk the wrong path. You often find The Corrector at a crossroads. Be patient. You will be rewarded if you wait to see which path he or she takes. Any other path should be fine.

The Influencer is a lively walker, all smiles, waves, and friendly greetings, with a twinkle in the eye and a bounce in the step. Shoulders back, head high, and chest forward, this person has a confident, extroverted personality who likes nothing more than engaging with people. At least those people who acknowledge them for always being right. The Influencers include politicians and others who believe they can walk on water, and can usually be seen trailing a retinue of wide-eyed and gullible Supporters struggling to keep up. Non-Supporters wish The Influencer would take a long walk off a short pier.

Everyone knows The Multi-Tasker walk at a glance. This person not only walks and talks, but texts and chews gum too. The Multi-Tasker has a problem-solver personality, and is usually vigorously engaged in searching for problems to solve. Especially yours. The Multi-Tasker likes to believe they walk the talk. They don't.

LONG LIVE THE SUN

In a recent conversation, a casual acquaintance happened to mention to me that the sun will die in 3 ½ billion years. Just flat out dropped that little bombshell on me as nonchalantly as he might have told me that my shoelaces were untied. What do you say to something like that? Naturally the conversation got a bit awkward afterwards.

Anyway, I managed to get away from him by saying that we don't have much time to waste then, and immediately went home and did a little research. It turns out that what most scientists actually believe is that the sun will begin to die in about five billion years when it starts to run out of energy and turns into a white dwarf.

Now if you're anything like me, you just let that last statement turn over in your head for a bit. But after I recovered, I thought about my friend. There's nothing like having incomplete or erroneous information to make one look like a fool, and while I felt sorry for him on that account, I don't know as I wouldn't feel a bit foolish myself trying to deliver this new information to him. While five billion years isn't nearly as scary as 3 ½ billion years, and I can certainly relate to running out of energy the older I get, I don't quite know what to make of that business about the sun suddenly turning into a white dwarf.

At first I chalked it up to the scientists having a bit of fun, and began to imagine other things the sun might turn into, like a purple banana, or a calico cat. But then I remembered that scientists as a group are notorious for lacking a sense of humor. When an apple fell on Newton's head for instance, he didn't laugh it off, and it didn't knock him silly. Instead it knocked enough sense in him to come up with the idea of gravity. You or I might have joked about it at least not being a coconut or a five-pound papaya, and gotten laughs telling the story for the next week.

Thomas Edison was so humor deprived that he threatened to sue the cartoonist who drew him in his lab with an imaginary light bulb over his head to represent a brilliant idea, claiming science is 99% perspiration and only 1% inspiration. Maybe it would have been funnier if the cartoonist had pictured him sweating profusely while standing in a puddle, but something tells me he wouldn't have found that funny either.

Then I finally figured it out. Dying is really scary, and even scientists don't like to talk about the sun's passing. So they transferred their fears into something less threatening. Just as the rest of us might turn into a couch potato or a vegetable the closer we get to death, they say the sun will turn into a white dwarf. Who are we to criticize? It is certainly better than imagining our mighty, beloved sun first expanding into a massive, solar system devouring red giant before tearing itself violently apart and helplessly collapsing into a small, powerless white mass.

As for me, it kind of takes the edge off the whole subject if I stick with it turning into a purple banana.

CALLING GOD

Calling out to God, whether it be in desperation, in sorrow, in thankfulness, or in flagrante delicto, couldn't be easier, and would appear to be the best way we have of getting His attention. But does He listen? I don't mean to question His capabilities, but I have to wonder. After all, there are billions of God worshipping people on this planet, and only one of Him, as far as we know. Now I may struggle with math, and with my belief too to be honest, but numbers don't lie, and those just don't add up. If He listens at all, I believe He would have to have a method of screening the calls so that He could just tune in to those of interest to Him.

So just for a moment, pretend that you are God. It's not difficult, sitting in judgment of other people is one of our most accomplished traits. We may not be able to go so far as to condemn another to Hell, but it's not for lack of trying. Anyway, as God, which of the above calls would be most likely to get YOUR attention? Receiving gratitude is always nice, especially for all that You do, or all that humans think You do, and requires no follow-up action on your part. This cannot be said about the burden of responsibility heaped on your broad shoulders by one needy whiner after another, day in and day out, year after year, on and on, world without end.

But c'mon. Be honest. Those calls from bed would HAVE to be the best part of your day, right? One would think humans would be mortified to know that their Lord and Savior was watching them in such delicate moments, but as neither Hell nor high water would ever get them to stop, that apparently is not the case. So, either they are exhibitionists looking for your approval of what they've done with their God given talents, or they don't know you're watching.

Either way, one thing becomes apparent. YOU LIKE TO WATCH! Possibly even set the whole thing up just for that purpose, and whatever else happens, war, hunger, the rape of Mother Nature, happens. Perhaps earth is nothing more than God's Private Peep Show. It is written that on the seventh day, the day after You created humans, You rested. It appears more and more likely that that is when You GOT BUSY! We will definitely NOT speculate on THAT however. You, the most private and secretive of beings, should understand more than anyone that we all deserve a little privacy, especially in our most intimate moments.

(Please God, if You're listening to this, I strongly suggest that You tune in to one of the other categories of callers. The show's over.)

ROOM FOR ONE

My mind is always open.
I'm glad that you inquired.
But there's only room for one,
And an appointment is required.

Did you file an application?
Have you paid the entrance fee?
Did you talk with other people
Before you came to me?

I know the wait is getting long,
But security is tight.
I can't admit just anyone.
Did you first try and write?

My mind is always open
But let there be no doubt,
If you insist on coming in,
Then I'll be stepping out.

WHO'S SMARTER?

My smart phone gives me the world,
Yet I feel like the martyr.
I give my life to it,
But don't feel any smarter.

THINK THOSE POUNDS AWAY

Are you tired of trying to lose weight and only losing your mind? Fed up with all the repackaged diet fads that make fat cats out of their promoters but only leave you hungry for donuts? Worn out from trying those insane exercise regimens delivered by over-caffeinated TV gurus? Well stop sweating it and use your head. I mean it. Literally. Play chess instead. The pounds will disappear like pawns in the Queen's gambit.

Scientists who study such things (and really, is there anything that scientists don't study?) say that chess professionals burn 6,000 calories per day in tournaments, which is right up there with active athletes. So you can't see yourself as a tournament caliber professional? Does a playground hoopster expend any less energy because she is not a pro playing for the WNBA championship? (Okay, so I just checked with the scientists and apparently found something they haven't studied. They say they'll get right on it.) But I'll put their reputation on the line and say no, of course not. Why would she, the activity is the same.

The average adult woman expends about 2000 calories in a typical day. For men it's about 2500. Of this, the brain alone accounts for 20 percent of the body's energy use, and that's just for doing the normal things that regulate the heart, lungs, and other organs we ignore, while it busies itself thinking about more important things like what TV programs to watch. But chess is not a normal thing, which is why under no circumstances should you leave your brain alone in front of a chess board for an extended period of time. Unless you are a professional, or you have something against your brain. Take it slowly.

In 2004, Rustam Kasimdzhanov gained the world championship but lost 17 pounds and I believe the lucrative endorsements of his vodka and pirozhki sponsors. Defending champ Anatoly Karpov lost 22 pounds in 1984, and nearly suffered the ignominy of being forced down to the light heavyweight class. In 2018, a U.S. fitness company monitored players during a tournament and found that grandmaster Mikhail Antipov burned 560 calories in two hours, the equivalent of what Roger Federer would burn in an hour of tennis. And he didn't need to wear a sweat band doing it. He should have stopped there, but you know chess players when they get excited. (Actually I don't, but maybe you do.) Watching television, by contrast, would burn 112 calories in the same period, unless you were watching a chess tournament, in which case I would have to consult the scientists again. But you see the possibilities.

In the interests of full disclosure, I write this as a 160-pound male who, for reasons unclear to me, couldn't gain weight on a diet of cheesecake and beer. Believe me, I've tried it. And neither do I play chess. Don't hate me. I do consider myself a professional level daydreamer however, so maybe it's time I give the scientists something else to look into.

BATS – BE A FRIEND, NOT AFRAID

Experts say there are some 1400 species of bats in the world. Many non-experts say that is about 1400 species too many. Those would likely include the chiroptophobiacs, the ones suffering from an irrational fear of bats, and the sanguivoriphobiacs, those suffering from an even more irrational fear of vampires. There are also people living in the American tropics that suffer a somewhat more rational fear of vampire bats. Presumably those people are called sanguivorichiroptophobiacs, a word which, if real, would scare me a lot more than any bat or vampire possibly could.

All those bats are divided into two main groups, the megabats and the microbats. If you want to know the difference, you'll have to look closely. There are few people who do so voluntarily. Those people are called batty. Mostly though the differences are a matter of size, which can range from two inches to nearly big enough to carry you away; and diet, which can range from vegetarian to blood thirsty. Fortunately, 70% of them only eat insects. They can have them. It might be why they look like they do. Imagine your own face if you had to eat nothing but insects.

One look at the face of any bat will tell you why there are no cuddly bat toys for children. Instead they get relegated to being horror movie and Halloween fright props. This is unfortunate. Not all animals can be the stars of the show like pandas and koalas, even though those are merely one-dimensional creatures that do nothing but look cute and eat bamboo shoots and eucalyptus leaves all day. You won't see the likes of them flying, hanging upside down, scaring people, and doing any of the fun things bats do.

Just because bats are ugly though doesn't mean we should call them names, but what are we supposed to do when so many of their actual names include degrading taunts like hog-nosed, funnel-eared, ghost-faced, leaf-nosed, wrinkle-lipped, hollow-faced, and hammer-headed? I'd like to see what the bat namers looked like, and take a shot at renaming them myself.

Bats make their homes everywhere except for the coldest parts of the Earth, and make up one-fifth of the total mammalian population. Yes, bats are mammals, and they are not flying rats. In fact, humans are more closely related to bats than to rats. Some more than others, I believe. Like humans, when they are not eating or sleeping, bats spend most of their time grooming or socializing. Most evolved to do so upside down in dark caves, adding a degree of difficulty to what humans only attempt to do in nightclubs.

Nine species of bats can be found in Connecticut, if anyone is looking for them. I prefer to let them stay hidden where they are. The most common are the little brown bats and the big brown bats, which must have been named after all the other derogatory bat names had been taken. These bats feed on mosquitos and agricultural pests such as cutworm and corn borer moths. They are among the bats that are estimated to save the agriculture industry in the U.S. many billions of dollars annually. And along with snakes and spiders, I believe the psychotherapy business owes them a big debt of gratitude as well.

All kidding aside, many species of bats need our help. In Connecticut, the U.S., and beyond, populations are threatened with extinction due to white nose syndrome, a devastating disease caused by a cold weather fungus that attacks them while they are hibernating. Bats are essential to the health of our shared environment, in part through seed dispersal, pollination, and insect control. They are not aggressive, will not fly into your hair, and most assuredly cannot turn you into a vampire. Like most mammals however, they can carry rabies, though it is quite rare. As with all wildlife, it is best to admire them from a distance, particularly at dusk, when they showcase their uniquely evolved echolocation talents in acrobatic insect hunts.

So be a real Batman or Batwoman superhero and put up bat houses and limit pesticide use. Learn more ways to help by visiting bat conservation web sites, and the CT DEEP Wildlife Division Bat Program web site at deep.batprogram@ct.gov.

GOLF - THE THRILL IS GONE

The worst thing about golf is that it takes about five hours to play a full round, give or take a few hours. And that's only if you don't keep score. Personally I prefer to just approximate. But strangely enough, it is also the best thing. Where else can you drive around at a slow, safe speed with a feeling approaching mild abandon, while drinking beers, and swearing mightily for hours on end? There are good reasons for the laws that prohibit this sort of behavior on the roadways. But I think that if some wise entrepreneurs were to come along and provide golf cart rentals and large fields without golf holes we could do away with the game entirely and never look back. Keep the sand traps and the water hazards however, and add in whatever obstacles you can think of that might ratchet up the thrill factor. (Bison and alligators come to my mind, but my mind does have its detractors.)

One thing I think we can all agree that golf lacks is a thrill factor. (If I'm going to start listing golf's shortcomings, I won't get out of this article till next week, so I'll try and just stick to this one because it already came up.) One look at any golfer will tell you how seriously thrill deprived he or she is. Much of this can be traced back to the aura of culture and privilege that the golf world cultivated so carefully since they wrested it from its free-spirited Scottish inventors so long ago. (It's either a little-known fact or a very old joke that those original Scottish course designers made the game eighteen holes because that's how long it took them to finish a bottle of whiskey.)

A recent Swedish study concluded that golfers live five years longer than non-golfers. They say it's because in Sweden most golfers walk, but let's face the facts here. In Sweden one can only walk for at most a month and a half a year. The rest of the time they're golfing from snowmobiles while experiencing hypothermia and frostbite thrills their American cart riding counterparts can't appreciate. So that's where the real longevity impact must come from. One must feel for the Swedes though if those extra five years must be spent playing golf. Walking might help the player some, even if it's only for a month and a half, but at what cost if it kills the game. Nobody has ever walked anywhere for the thrill of it.

There is a chance yet to save both the game of golf from obsolescence and golfers from flatlining. The golf moguls must each come down from Mount Augusta and either bring back the old Scottish spirits, or find the inner child they left behind on the miniature golf courses, athletic fields, and amusement parks of their youth. Golf should be fun. They must hire young, imaginative new course designers that bring out the best of these worlds. Throw out the stupor inducing 168-page PGA rulebook and the even larger rule interpretation book and make some new rules that allow players to subtract strokes for swearing creativity, most lost balls found, longest golf cart skids, and the like. Have designated polo holes where players must hit the balls from their carts. While moving. Or for even more thrills, make it a polo like competition with two person teams each in a cart vying for control of one ball. There are eighteen holes and hundreds of yards per hole in which to be creative.

The game of golf and the very life blood of golfers depend on it.

OUR MINDS
WHOSE SIDE ARE THEY ON?

We all like to believe that we know our own minds. After all, they are our minds, minds we grew up with, whether they grew with us or not. Despite the neglect and abuse, our minds have remained as constant as a pet dog, always there to serve us. Sure, what it serves us might only be the mental equivalent of a threadbare, chewed up tennis ball, but at least we can still recognize it for what it is. Or can we?

Social psychologists are here to tell us that we don't know our minds as well as we think we do, especially when they're anywhere in the proximity of other minds. And they have the experiments to prove it. Now, I'm willing to bet that most of your minds are already giving you some grief over where this seems to be going. A mind fears nothing more than a psychologist, and even a pet dog can bolt if it smells a rat. Who wants to believe their mind could be deceiving them? But I urge you to try and keep your mind engaged the best you can. You will need it for this. Personally, I find that when my mind is threatened, a few kind words and a stiff drink works better than beating my head against the wall to show it who's boss. Feels better too.

Psychologist Stanley Milgram, in his famous obedience experiments following WWII, discovered that people would knowingly, if reluctantly, be willing to deliver a potentially fatal electric shock to a test subject when ordered to by an authority figure. I'm sure you're all thinking no, my mind wouldn't let me do that. Just remember that it's our minds that are doing the thinking, so of course they would think that. But you have to wonder when they won't even let us understand what 'mind' really is. Could it be the ultimate authority figure? I get the uneasy feeling that I could be in for a shock myself if I don't write what my mind tells me to.

In the "Violinist in the Metro Experiment", one of the world's most renowned violinists posed as a street musician, playing his concert repertoire in a subway station on his $3.5 million handcrafted instrument. Most people quickly hurried past. This experiment revealed to the researchers that our minds typically only recognize beauty when it is anticipated, or the setting is appropriate. Still, it was a violinist. Maybe it's just me, but I'd be willing to bet that our minds would do much better if given the chance against a world class accordionist.

In the "Stanford Prison Experiment", psychologist Philip Zimbardo discovered that participants placed in the role of prisoners became very stressed, undoubtedly because those placed in the role of guards increasingly began to abuse their power, so much so that the experiment had to be stopped after six days. I can relate to this. You should have seen how my mind reacted when it only had to help me to guard a box of donuts for the office.

The donuts never stood a chance. Apparently our minds are not to be trusted in positions of power.

So much for independent minds. In Solomon Asch's conformity experiments, people were asked to determine which of three lines was longest. When the first people intentionally picked the wrong line, the following people were more likely to choose the same one. Regarding this experiment, I'm compelled to ask if Mr. Asch ever conferred with Mr. Zimbardo. I'm a bit skeptical that our minds could be Attila the power-mad Hun one minute, and Stanley Milquetoast the next, afraid of standing up for what we believe to be true? Before I decide however, I'm going to wait and see what other people think about this.

In the "Carlsberg Social Experiment," a movie theater was nearly filled with people dressed to look like intimidating bikers. Most unsuspecting movie goers turned around and left, revealing how our minds make snap judgements based on appearances. I have yet to figure out why most people walk away from me however, as I look like Brad Pitt. I'm starting to feel that my mind and I might have a dishonest relationship. Whenever I feed it information, I believe it just pretends to process it before telling me what I want to hear.

In the "Robbers Cave Experiment," psychologist Muzafer Sherif and his team placed twenty-two boys in two groups, neither of which was aware of the other. The boys bonded with each other during the first week, then were placed in direct competition with the other group. Intergroup conflict was the result, with the boys favoring their own group members and disparaging the others. This experiment shows that when our minds find themselves in a group, they will do what they can to validate it, as long as they have other minds to demonize. Now I don't want to start a fight or anything, especially since my mind is not a part of any group at the moment, but might not a group of psychologist's minds do what it can to validate itself also? Just saying.

Excuse me, but I have to apologize. I also meant to cover the "Piano Stairs Experiment," the "Smoky Room Experiment," the "False Consensus Experiment," and the "Halo Effect Experiment," but my mind is telling me that I've gone too far and have to end this article now, calling it the "Slanderous Writer's Experiment." See what I have to deal with?

DESTINY - THE LEGEND

Legend has it that sometime after Destiny was born, she looked around and decided that there had to be an easier way to go through life. She noticed that humans paid tribute to all sorts of Gods, but that for their sacrifice, they expected something in return. That meant work for the Gods. She wondered if there was a way to exact tribute without working.

Over time she came up with the idea of a pre-ordained path, a beautiful tree and flower lined path that led to wondrous places. She figured people would gladly pay whatever small toll she imposed to travel such a path. But she soon noticed that while good people were willing to pay a tribute to use it, if she wasn't there to collect it, bad people would also go through to these magnificent places without paying. Destiny was furious. Creating a pre-ordained path took effort, and she deserved to be compensated. So she created a second path, an ugly, difficult path that led through torment and misery. If bad people didn't want to pay her, she figured, then let them suffer for their choice. But damned if she would suffer a loss of revenue, so she raised the toll on the first path and increased her oversight, which made her very unhappy.

What Destiny noticed then however was yet another adjustment in the traffic on her pathways. Now only people who could afford her toll, whether good or bad, travelled the path of wonders. And that those people who could not afford to pay were crowding in ever growing numbers onto the path of suffering.

Destiny was no fool. If she wanted an easy life, she certainly knew how to achieve it now. She raised the toll again. Still people paid. In fewer numbers to be sure, but her toll collection work was reduced for the same dividend. So she raised it still further, and even began to accept extremely lucrative bribes from those who wanted to create their own paths. Destiny just smiled and ordained the new paths. If rich people wanted to buy her off, she was fine with that. It meant even less work for her.

The hordes that crammed onto the path of suffering swelled further. The path degraded century by century, and it could no longer carry everyone easily. People were jostled off the path, or simply left it, and so created new paths of suffering. Destiny just smiled, marveled at the new ways people could find to suffer, and ordained the new paths as quickly as they were created. At least she didn't have to create them. Her workload had been successfully reduced to the bare minimum of ordaining new paths, which she could now practically do in her sleep.

It has been said that Destiny is a lazy, greedy, sadistic bitch, who frowns on the poor and smiles on the rich. That is not true. She smiles on everyone.

GALILEO GALILEI

Galileo Galilei,
Yearned to see the grand display
Of astronomical delights,
Appearing closer in his sights.

And so he made a telescope,
And raised it up quite full of hope.
His neighbor though thought him a spy,
And showed a moon not in the sky.

THE TRAFFIC

(with apologies to William Blake)

Traffic! Traffic! Burning gas,
On the highways nose to ass,
What deranged, sadistic mind
Would jam commuters to this grind?

In what deepest darkest hells
Burns the poisons thou expels?
On what tires dare He roll?
What the wheel that lost control?

And what tolls, what breakdown lanes,
Could speed the neurons of thy brain?
And when thy brain should overheat,
What dread voice? On what dread street?

What the road rage? What the gun?
In whose brain should I put one?
What the horn? What baseball bat
Dares the driver to combat?

When the drivers shout their jeers
And ram the others, sides and rears,
Did He smile his work to see?
Does He run the DMV?

Traffic! Traffic! Burning gas,
On the highways nose to ass,
What deranged sadistic mind
Would jam commuters to this grind?

TRYST AT THE TRUST

(based on a true story)

I read that in Kenya at the Wildlife Trust,
Two distinct species felt an uncommon lust,
When a wild Grevey's zebra and an amorous donkey,
Became acquainted and produced a zonkey.
It had stripes on its legs and a donkey's pride,
But was not black and white, on either side.

The caretakers struggled to believe their own eyes,
And began to think that their Trust was unwise.
Because hybrids like this weren't supposed to exist!
And if they kept their Trust, who'd be next to tryst?
They looked at the elephant first. Then the rhino.
Could they be relephant? Elephino.

THE BUTTERFLY WHAT'S IN A NAME

It's butterfly season as I write this, and the gardens look as delighted as I am at the return of these ethereal creatures. Not one of them however reminds me of either a dairy product or a pestilent insect. So how then did the butterfly come by its odd name?

The leading theories take us back to merry old England, where most of the butterflies were yellow or cream colored. Add to this the observation that they often hovered around butter churns and milk pails, and you get all the reinforcement you need for the ancient belief that witches would turn themselves into these magical creatures in order to fly off with the butter. (Witches, for their part, realized that the people who believed this were the same people who turned themselves into hysterical idiots at anything they didn't understand, all the more so as their potions never included butter.)

The upshot of all this was the Old English word buter-flēoge, which rather obviously combines the words butter and flēoge. As people tired of trying to pronounce flēoge, which meant any flying animal, the word eventually metamorphosed into fly, for any flying insect. Butterflies have been enchanting the gardens of English speaking folk ever since, who, with the modernization of the dairy industry, have reported no further problems with disappearing butter. In an ironic twist, witches, however, have been complaining of late about modern farming practices being responsible for the scarcity of eye of newt and toe of frog.

In an obvious attempt to raise these elegant creatures above their natural order, the Danes and Norwegians call butterflies sommerfugls, which means summer birds. It's a nice try, but it doesn't change the fact that they are bugs, not birds. (If you happen to see a bird with six legs, compound eyes, and antennae, please let me know.) What they should work on changing is the word fugl, which does no justice at all to the wonder and beauty of birds.

In Russia, butterflies are called babochka, which translates to "little souls". Many cultures in fact took their linguistic cues from the ancient Greeks, who called a butterfly "Psyche", which means soul, based on the belief that our souls go to heaven as butterflies when we die. Now a heaven full of butterflies sounds beautiful, but I wonder if those ancient Greeks knew that butterflies lay eggs. A heaven crawling with caterpillars should be enough to make any soul ponder the alternatives.

The Greeks may have thought they had soul transportation figured out, but as entomologists remind us, most butterflies only live for 3 – 4 weeks and fly 12 mph at top speed. And that's without the added burden of carrying a human soul. This puts heaven at most 6 - 8,000 miles away, which is far below the orbit of GPS and TV satellites. By any theological measure this would seem to be a gross miscalculation. By any entomological measure, the delicate wings of butterflies were never meant for the transportation of human souls, at least not much beyond the garden.

The German word for butterfly is schmetterling, which, terrifyingly enough, may come from the word schmettern, meaning "to smash". I would steer clear of Germany if I was a butterfly. The Dutch call these amazing insects vlinders, which describes the yellowish color of butterfly excrement. Sorry, I didn't see that one coming. You would think that the people who brought us Rembrandt and the rest of the Dutch Masters would have been more drawn to the vibrancy of the creature itself than to its waste products.

The best poets could not have come up with lovelier names for the butterfly than mariposa (Spain), papillon (France), and farfalla (Italy). Mariposa means the Virgin Mary at rest. I don't see it, but since butterflies could be perceived as the living embodiment of Rorschacht ink blot psychological tests, I suppose they can look like anything to anybody. Papillon and farfalla are lifted from the Latin. Don't ask. Even thinking about Latin makes my heart flutter as erratically as the flight of a butterfly.

On a sad note, butterfly populations across the globe are declining rapidly, and it has nothing to do with the names they're called. They're not THAT sensitive. They are sensitive though to habitat loss, climate change, and other environmental stressors. I hope we can all comprehend this, and soon, because butterflies are a critical pollination link in the food chain. (How sensitive do you think we would be if we were forced from our homes, the grocery stores all closed, and the farmer's crops all died off a little more each year?)

Whatever we call butterflies, we would not want to have to call them extinct. We could never take it back.

(Please check butterfly conservation web sites for things we can all do to help.)

THE DIFFERENCE BETWEEN FROGS, HERONS, AND NOVELISTS

Let us begin by going back a million or so years to view a scene that would not be out of place today, a frog sitting on a lily pad near the shoreline of a small, weedy pond. The frog intermittently croaks its urgent message to the world, then lapses into a waiting, watchful silence. Eventually another frog answers by climbing up onto the lily pad, whereupon the first frog wastes no time in climbing onto its back. After a few moments they separate, and the second frog swims away. Having been preoccupied, however, the first frog never notices the heron, and resumes croaking. This time the heron answers, by devouring the frog in a lightning flash of its rapier bill.

Now let us imagine an early hominid watching this life and death drama from the shore, feeling sad to see the frog's life come to such a brutal end and pondering, in its early hominid way, the Great Mystery of Life, asking itself, "Who am I?" "Why am I here?" and "What happens after I die?" Of course no one will ever know exactly what the hominid may have been thinking, not only because it was a million years ago, but also because at such a moment a saber-toothed tiger likely would have pounced on any hominid so distracted with pointless questions.

For a split second the hominid may have realized that it should have been more aware, and that any randy frog or hungry heron will reveal to you the Story of Life if you are observant. 'It's not a mystery,' the frog croaks beguilingly. 'But it is a short story,' acknowledges the heron, struggling to swallow the whole frog, story and all. 'Eat, survive, reproduce, die,' chants the creature chorus, eyeballing each other warily. A rather bleak story perhaps, but a story that had up until then been nonetheless bought without question by every single creature that had ever existed over the millions of years of life on this planet. In fact, you could have called this story a runaway best seller.

The problem though with runaway best sellers is, they eventually run away. And after many thousands of years had passed, this one did. Because from those dark chapters stepped a new sort of hominid, Homo Sapiens, the Wise Human. And suddenly the story's not selling. "The plot is weak," some Wise Humans said. "Character development is nonexistent," said others. "And that ending, well, that ending is simply unacceptable," they all agreed. "Nobody would ever buy it. Where's the motivation? Where's the imagination? We need more!" they cried. "Rewrite the script!"

And so the script was rewritten, then revised a thousand times a thousand with ever changing characters, plots, purposes, and endings until the original story could be found only in the croak of a frog, or the flash of a heron's bill. But still the Wise Humans were not satisfied. For each of them believed that they alone possessed the one true script, and that all others were silly misunderstandings at best, perfidious lies at worst, and it was therefore incumbent on them to point this out by any means necessary.

Incredible as it may seem however, from time to time a few Wise Humans arrive on this Carousel of Beliefs with ambiguous scripts, scripts so replete with mystery and uncertainty that their bewildered owners are kept dizzy by all the carnival barkers looking to pounce on them with their sweet promises of the rides of a lifetime. These vulnerable humans are called Novelists, and their stories are the stuff of tears, laughter, passion, and much soul-searching.

Frogs are still called frogs however, and herons are still herons, and both remain as far removed from the Carousel of Beliefs as can be. Unlike the Novelists, they have all continued to have faith in the original script, and don't give it a second thought.

ARE THE TREES BEING SILENCED?

On a scale from fungi to humans, how smart do you think trees are? Canadian Dr. Suzanne Simard and German forester Peter Wohlleben, who know a thing or two about trees, believe they're smarter than most animals. Personally, I never doubted that some trees were smart, I just figured it depended on the type of tree and the environment in which it was raised. The bald cypress and the swamp maple for instance never struck me as particularly intelligent, but what can you expect when they grow up with bugs, snakes, and swamp scum. You will never see the American beech, the Sitka spruce, or the Imperial palm hanging out with the likes of those trees. They practically lord their magisterial intelligence over any landscape they inhabit. They have things to tell us, if we could but understand them.

Turns out we can, we just haven't been listening to them like Dr. Simard and Mr. Wohlleben have. They say that trees use chemical, hormonal, and electrical signals to cooperate with each other and maintain relationships, to transfer nutrients to neighboring trees in need, and significantly, to warn each other about environmental concerns heading their way. They do all this through underground, symbiotic networks of soil fungi, and they say we should be paying attention to the messages they have for humans.

Before you question why trees don't tell us their messages more directly if they're so darn important, instead of using some oddball tree whisperers to deliver them, well, they've tried that and have apparently concluded that fungi listen better than humans. This is not surprising, given that fungi are very like many humans, only closer to the ground. Here is the short history of tree communication as I was able to determine:

The Sumerian God of Wisdom, Ea, was said to embody the cedar tree. Whether that was such a wise move for a God can be debated, but when the trees started delivering prophesies, the people listened. At least for a while. As the Sumerians were overthrown by the Babylonians however, either the prophesies were bad or the people stopped listening, and neither the cedar trees nor Ea were ever heard from again.

In ancient Greece, Zeus considered the oak tree sacred, particularly one he was fond of in the Grove of Selloi, and authorized it to give prophesies. It went over so well that he gave the same permission to all the oaks in the grove, and in a generous move, to the beeches as well. This was asking for trouble. Priests and priestesses were soon overwhelmed with prophesies to interpret. Some favored the oak, and some the beeches, and conflict ensued as the trees' messages blurred. Prophesies may have no longer borne fruit, but the trees continued to bear nuts for many years.

That was the last time trees were heard from directly, though their attempts to communicate their concerns to us didn't stop. From time to time, prophets would recognize the wisdom trees had to impart, and would sit under them for hours to learn all they could. Being prophets, they didn't reveal their methods. This worked well where you had a particularly enlightened prophet involved, like the Buddha, but more often than not second-rate prophets would pick the less intelligent trees to sit under, with the predictable result that second-rate information would get passed along. This didn't benefit either the humans or the trees, only the fungal network.

If you sensed a sudden, sinister chill crawl up your back, pay attention. Trees are reliant on fungal networks to communicate with each other, and to communicate their warnings to those of us who would listen. Fungi, therefore, control all messaging. Now ask yourself what motivates fungi. In case you don't know, it's death. They get stronger when everything around them is dead or dying. And as humans continue to plunder the earth and slide ever nearer to an apocalypse, we still are not getting the trees' messages of environmental concern. Meanwhile, fungi grow bigger and stronger. The largest living organism on earth is not the blue whale. It's a fungus covering four square miles that is slowly killing the trees.

Perhaps fungi should be sitting atop the intelligence scale.

DOLPHINS VS. SHARKS

Everybody loves dolphins. No, that's not the name of a new television show, but it should be. Dolphins are intelligent, charismatic creatures with a camera-ready smile that seems to be always asking the question, "Are you my friend?" Sharks get a whole week of TV dedicated to them and what do they have to offer? Nothing but big teeth and a stone cold look that, if it asks any question at all, it's "Are you my dinner?"

Being complex animals, it seems only fitting that dolphins have a complex evolutionary history. Fifty million years ago they were four-legged mammals that were apparently already smart enough to realize that the world was ¾ ocean, and that what the oceans really needed were some mammals to give them a bit of class. Fish were clearly only going to take the oceans so far, especially since all of the smarter ones had quit them for the land 325 million years earlier. These had gotten busy evolving into amphibians, reptiles, birds, and mammals, and many could already demonstrate such advanced behaviors as caring for their young instead of eating them. The time was ripe to return home.

Ever so slowly then, one line of mammals became amphibious, much like the modern hippopotamus, which is believed to be the dolphin's closest living relative. Thinking it could do better than that, and really, who couldn't, it took the final plunge about forty million years ago and eventually became the dolphin we all know and love.

The oceans may have been without mammals in those early days, but what the new dolphins didn't know was that the oceans were most definitely not devoid of sharks. And that these sharks had already survived five mass extinction events over their 450 million years of existence in large part because they were not picky eaters. They also did not think much of evolution, particularly after discovering these strange new interlopers with their big brains and their fancy manners who did not show the proper fear and respect at mealtimes.

Dolphins, in fact, have the second largest brain to body mass ratio to humans, and while sharks may have the largest fish brains, they're still just fish brains, and I don't think anybody has ever been impressed by a fish's thoughts with the exception of certain fishermen. You know who you are. Anyway, it likely did not take the dolphins long to take the measure of sharks. When they saw that sharks never slept, as they had to constantly swim to push water over their gills to breathe, the dolphins didn't just wait to be eaten in their sleep. They evolved the amazing ability to shut down half their brain so as to let the other half keep things running smoothly. (A word of caution is warranted here. These are professional dolphins. Any humans operating in half brain mode should think twice about continuing, or risk serious injury to everything they hold dear.)

Incredibly, dolphins exhibit culture, shared patterns of thought, language, and behaviors that allow them to form complex societies. They also use tools, typically shells and sponges. Sharks lack culture, as anybody knows who has seen them eat. They do not even much like other sharks, and sharing an ocean is about as far as they will go. The only tools they use are their own teeth, which, while impressive for biting prospective food, and really just about anything because everything looks like prospective food to them, are rather limited.

Dolphins in the U.S. and Russian Navies for instance have even been trained to use cameras, spears, and explosives, though both the dolphins and the governments would probably deny it. Sharks, who have been found with such things in their stomachs as fur coats, cannonballs, tires, and a whole suit of armor, would undoubtedly eat even the explosives. Any denials would be loud, but pointless.

Most scientists who study dolphins, or cetologists, agree that dolphins are intelligent on the basis that they can understand new situations, apply newly learned knowledge, and think abstractly. They also note that dolphins demonstrate self-awareness, problem-solving, grief, empathy, joy, teaching skills, and playfulness. Most dolphins say the same things about cetologists, with the exception of those cetologists affiliated with dolphin shows. Dolphins know when anyone is operating with only half a brain.

Dolphins say these things because they can. Through a wide variety of whistles, yelps, squeaks, clicks, and behaviors, their communication abilities are extensive and complex. Bottlenose dolphins are the most widely studied species, and cetologists believe that all bottlenose dolphins have a distinctive whistle, called a signature whistle, which identifies each individual like a name. Infants learn their names from their mothers, and keep them for life.

Sharks demonstrate hunger. They make no sounds, communicating primarily through biting, which does often elicit loud sounds from those bitten. If 450 million years of shark evolution have not produced any of the signs of intelligence of a dolphin, it's probably pointless to wait. Still, there is Shark Week, which, while good for the sharks, may actually say something more about human than shark intelligence. (Nine out of ten dolphins thought this was funny. The tenth was busy watching Shark Week.)

THE DOOMSDAY DANCE

Apocalypses, as a rule, or even as a hint, suggestion, or threat, would not ordinarily seem to offer much opportunity for hope. But humans are a strange lot, and often find hope in the strangest places. The first swallows returning to Capistrano. The first baby born to a new year. The first daffodils in the spring. The first sign that anyone is paying attention to the Doomsday Clock.

The Doomsday Clock, in case you haven't heard the ticking, is not your ordinary, side-of-the-bed alarm clock that typically starts our days. It is not an alarm clock that you want to wake up to. A Monday is bad enough, but a Doomsday? As you might guess from the name, its intention is to wake us up to the end of our days, which is more alarming than a lifetime of Mondays. Should you be wondering, it would pretty much end our nights too, which by my calculations wouldn't leave us much to work with.

You might think that such an alarming alarm clock would come with a very prominent snooze button, but you'd be wrong. The scientists who developed and now maintain the Doomsday Clock say its existence is due to the fact that we've been snoozing since its creation in 1947. Seventy-four years is a long time to snooze. Rip van Winkle had a twenty year cat nap by comparison and he missed the American Revolution. I suppose one can always hope that we'll snooze long enough to miss Doomsday, but something tells me that it would be a poor strategy to try sleeping our way through a world ending apocalypse.

Those early scientists behind the Doomsday Clock included Albert Einstein and some members of the Manhattan Project, who not only developed the world's first nuclear weapons, but also found a way to finally open Pandora's Box in the process. Unfortunately, the first tests of those weapons have made it hard to even find the remains of Pandora's Box, never mind to put it back together and close it again. The scientists believed that the creation of the Doomsday Clock was the next best option. I think Pandora would have approved.

When the Doomsday Clock was first devised back in 1947, the scientists set it at seven minutes to midnight, a symbolic representation of how close they believed we were to the end of the dance. I'm not talking about the hokey-pokey here, though to be fair, the way the clock has moved since then gives the appearance that we're first stepping in, then stepping out, then shaking it all about. All while it moves inexorably towards midnight. In 1953, for instance, the clock was moved to two minutes before midnight due to heightened U.S. – USSR nuclear tensions, then back to six minutes to midnight in 1973 because of peacekeeping actions by the United Nations. It's believed that the U.N. felt at that time that both parties were shaking it all about a bit too much.

Now it's 2021, and the scientists have set the clock at 100 seconds to midnight. If you're wondering where the time went, it seems we stopped to pick up a few more existential threats to humanity on the way – climate change, a pandemic, cyber-enabled information warfare, and the deliberate erosion of science by politicians – all new passengers on the Oblivion Express. "The number of ways in which we walk blithely into Armageddon is very high," said one of the scientists, who adds, rather un-blithely, "Agitate for change! It's not too late!"

I don't know about you, but 100 seconds to midnight doesn't seem like enough time to even do the hokey-pokey. We can try, but how many chances will we have to step out again? It seems to me that if we're to have any hope at all that we'll wake up before our dance is over, it's that perhaps the scientists forgot to consider daylight savings time. That at least would shine more light on the Doomsday Clock, and stand a chance of finally getting some people's attention. If not, it still could give us another hour to add a tap dance to our repertoire before the curtain comes down.

BIBLIOGRAPHY

The Complete History of Mankind

Little, Becky. "How Did Humans Evolve". History Magazine, 5 March 2020, www.history.com

"Evolution of Modern Humans". 13 June 2016, www.yourgenome.org

"Neanderthal vs. Cro-Magnon: What's the Difference?". 6 September 2016, www.mentalfloss.com

Barras, Colin. "We Don't Know Which Species Should be Classified as Human". BBC, January 2016, www.bbc.com

Coyotes – Get Used to Them

Twain, Mark. Roughing It. Sea Wolf Press, 2018

Bradford, Alina. "Coyote Facts". 2 April 2021, www.livescience.com

Lariviere, Serge. "Coyote – Description, Size, Habitat, and Facts". Britannica, www.britannica.com

Brain Wars – The Gender Variations

Price, Michael. "Study Finds Some Significant Differences in Brains of Men and Women". Science Magazine, April 2017, www.sciencemag.org

Oster, Emily. "Do Men and Women Have Different Brains?". The New York Times, 9 September 2019, www.nytimes.com

Edmunds, Molly. "Do Men and Women Have Different Brains". 8 October 2008, https://science.howstuffworks.com

"The 8 Differences Between Male and Female Brains". Great Performers, https://greatperformersacademy.com

Animal Arsonists

Gabbert, Bill. "Bear Falls on Sheriff's Vehicle Causing Crash and Fire". Wildfire Today, 9 August 2019, https://wildfiretoday.com

Greshko, Michael. "Why These Birds Carry Flames in their Beaks". National Geographic, 8 January 2018, www.nationalgeographic.com

"Great Chicago Fire". Wikipedia. Revised 26 April 2021, https://en.wikipedia.org

What Do We Have To Lose?

Grabianowski, Ed. "How Many Skin Cells Do You Shed Every Day?". 6 July 2010, https://health.howstuffworks.com
Menon, Meenambika. "51 Fun Facts About the Human Body, from a Science Teacher". The Indian Express, 31, July 2019, https://indiaexpress.com
Anderson, David and Hunt, Bob. "How Much Skin, Blood, and Saliva the Human Body can Make in a Lifetime". Business Insider, 8 September 2020, www.businessinsider.com

Do Birds Think?

Aristotle. The History of Animals
Hance, Jeremy. "Birds are More Like 'Feathered Apes' than 'Bird Brains'". The Guardian, 5 November 2016, www.theguardian.com
Stymacks, Amelia. "Ravens, Crows, Parrots, and More – Meet the Most Intelligent Birds". National Geographic, 15 March 2018, www.nationalgeographic.com

Take Your Mind for a Walk

Weiner, Eric. The Geography of Genius. Simon and Schuster, 2016
Jabr, Ferris. "Why Walking Helps Us Think". The New Yorker, 3 September 2014, www.newyorker.com
Weiner, Eric. The Geography of Bliss. Transworld Publishers Ltd, 2008

The Dirt on Forest Bathing

Fitzgerald, Sunny. "Forest Bathing: What it Is and Where to Do It". National Geographic, 18 October 2019, www.nationalgeographic.com
"Association of Nature and Forest Therapy Guides and Programs". 2020, www.natureandforesttherapy.org
Kim, Meeri. "Forest Bathing is Latest Fitness Trend to Hit U.S. – Where Yoga was 30 Years Ago". The Washington Post, 17 May 2017, www.washingtonpost.com

Dancing to Your Circadian Rhythm

Savvy, Jade Wu. "How to Survive as a Night Owl in a 9 – 5 World". Scientific American, 27 January 2020, www.scientificamerican.com
Sukel, Kayt. "Are People Really 'Morning Larks' or 'Night Owls'?". 14 October 2014, www.brainfacts.org

Jaffe, Eric. "Morning People vs. Night Owls: 9 Insights Backed by Science". 19 May 2015, www.fastcompany.com

The Age of Dogs

Wogan, Lisa. "Dog Aging Project Takes Veterinary Research in New Direction". VIN News Service, 28 October 2019, https://news.vin.com
Gorman, James. "Old Dogs, New Research, and the Secrets of Aging". The New York Times, 9 November 2020, www.nytimes.com
AKC Staff. "How to Calculate Dog Years to Human Years". American Kennel Club, 20 November 2019, www.akc.org

Boredom – It's Not Just for the Boring

Talbot, Margaret. "What Does Boredom do to Us – and for Us?". The New Yorker, 20 August 2020, www.newyorker.com
Stewart, Jude. "Boredom is Good for You". The Atlantic, June 2017, www.theatlantic.com
Rhodes, Ella. "The Exciting Side of Boredom". The British Psychological Society, April 2015, https://thepsychologist.bps.org.uk

World Migratory Bird Daze

Lorenzo, Irene. "Migration Marathons: 7 Unbelievable Bird Journeys". Bird Life International, 27 June 2018, www.birdlife.org
Lockhart, Jhaneel. "9 Awesome Facts about Bird Migration". Audubon, 11 October 2012, www.audubon.org
Ganninger, Daniel. "The World's Highest Flying Bird". 18 October 2020, https://medium.com

The Pursuit of Happiness Can Leave You Exhausted

Veenhoven, Ruut. The World Database of Happiness. Erasmus University Rotterdam, The Netherlands, https://worlddatabaseofhappiness.eur.nl
Weiner, Eric. The Geography of Bliss. Transworld Publishers Ltd, 2008
Brooks, Arthur C. "The Three Equations for a Happy Life, Even During a Pandemic". The Atlantic, 9 April 2020, www.theatlantic.com

Bonsai – The Abhorrent, Yet Artful, War on Trees

Simon, Wilbert. "How to Make a Bonsai Tree". Bonsai Tree Gardener, 22 September 2018, www.bonsaitreegardener.net

Nix, Steve. "Evolution of Forests and Trees". Treehugger, 3 September 2018, www.treehugger.com

DIY Brain Zapping

Jarrett, Christian. "Read This Before Zapping Your Brain". Wired, 20 January 2014, www.wired.com
"What is transcranial Direct Current Stimulation (tDCS)?". Neuromodec, https://neuromodec.com
"Galen – Biography, Facts, and Pictures". Famous Scientists, www.famousscientists.org

In Your Face

Engelhaupt, Erika. "Hundreds of Tiny Arachnids are Likely on Your Face Right Now". National Geographic, 23 April 2020, www.nationalgeographic.com

The Great Viking Makeover

Mackenzie, Laura. "20 Facts about Vikings". History Hit, 4 July 2018, www.historyhit.com
Goodrich, Ryan. "Viking History: Facts and Myths". 29 August 2019, www.livescience.com
Parker, Philip. "A Brief History of the Vikings". History Extra, 2016, www.historyextra.com

How Smart are Squirrels

"20 Fun Facts about Squirrels". Summit Environmental Solutions, www.summitenvironmentalsolutions.com
"Amazing Facts about the Squirrel". One Kind Planet, https://onekindplanet.org
Gibbens, Sarah. "Quirky Squirrel Behaviors You Can See This Fall". National Geographic, 10 October 2017, www.nationalgeographic.com
The Squirrel Lovers Club website, www.thesquirreloversclub.com
Bradford, Alina. "Squirrels: Diet, Habits, and Other Facts". 27 June 2014, www.livescience.com

Cloudy with a Chance of Daydreams

Day, Dr. John A. Cloudman website, www.cloudman.com

Cloud Appreciation Society website, https://cloudappreciationsociety.org
"Types of Clouds". National Oceanic and Atmospheric Administration, https://scijinks.gov/clouds
"7 Facts about Clouds". Met Office, www.metoffice.gov.uk
Mooallem, Jon. "The Amateur Cloud Society that (Sort of) Rattled the Scientific Community". The New York Times, 4 May 2016, www.nytimes.com

Brain Power

"Your Amazing Brain". National Geographic Kids, https://kids.nationalgeographic.com

Cat Research for Dummies

Grimm, David. "Cats Rival Dogs on Many Tests of Social Smarts. But is Anyone Brave Enough to Study Them?". Science Magazine, 9 May 2019, www.sciencemag.org
Newitz, Annalee. "Cats are an Extreme Outlier Among Domestic Animals". ARS Technica, 19 June 2017, https://arstechnica.com
Smith, Casey. "Cats Domesticated Themselves, Ancient DNA Shows". National Geographic, 19 June 2017, www.nationalgeographic.com
Rosen, Rebecca J. "How Humans Created Cats". The Atlantic, 16 December 2013, www.theatlantic.com

Classical Anatomy

Bellinger, Ines. "How Bach's Anatomy May have Handed Him Greatness". National Geographic, September 2019, www.nationalgeographic.com
Bennett, James II. "Weird Classical: When Schuman Ruined his Fingers". WXXR Editorial, 9 August 2017, www.wqxr.org
Meier, Allison. "Objects of Intrigue – Chopin's Immortal Hands". Atlas Obscura, 11 June 2014, www.atlasobscura.com

Collecting – A Hobby for Psychoanalysts

McKinley, Mark B. "The Psychology of Collecting". The National Psychologist, 31 May 2011, https://nationalpsychologist.com
"Psychology of Collecting". Wikipedia, Revised 26 March 2021, https://en.wikipedia.org

The Connecticut State Animal You've Never Seen

"Sperm Whale". National Geographic, www.nationalgeographic.com
"Sperm Whale – Facts, Pictures, and More about Sperm Whales". Oceanwide Expeditions, https://oceanwideexpeditions.com
Normen, Elizabeth J. "Why the Sperm Whale is Our State Animal". Connecticut Explored, Summer 2013, www.ctexplored.org

Food Fight at the Bird Feeder

Haigh, Alison. "When 136 Bird Species Show Up at a Feeder, Which One Wins?". Living Bird, Winter 2018, www.allaboutbirds.org
Durfee, Nell. "Who Wins the Feeder War?". Audubon, 1 February 2018, www.audubon.org
Wright, Jim. "The Bird Watcher: Pecking Order at the Bird Feeder". The Record, 2 November 2016, www.northjersey.com

Brain Farts – The Blame Game

"10 Everyday Things that Cause Brain Farts". 16 April 2012, www.livescience.com
Keany, Leeaundra. "Anatomy of a Brain Fart". Discover Magazine, 22 December 2009, www.discovermagazine.com

Are You Looking at Me?

Benn, Evan. "Casino Buys Virgin Mary Sandwich for $28,000". The Miami Herald, 23 November 2004, www.miamiherald.com

Fermenting Trouble – Animals and Alcohol

Muller, Natalie. "Animals Getting High:10 Common Drunks". Australian Geographic, 14 October 2011, www.australiangeographic.com
DeGraaf, Jack. "5 Animals that Get Drunk in the Wild". www.thefactsite.com
Zielinski, Sarah. "The Alcoholics of the Animal World". Smithsonian Magazine, 16 September 2011, www.smithsonianmag.com
Nuwer, Rachel. "Elephants Really Can't Hold Their Liquor". The New York Times, 20 May 2020, www.nytimes.com

Walk This Way

"What the Way You Walk Reveals About Your Personality". https://brightside.me

Wanshel, Elyse. "The Way You Walk Reveals THIS About Your Personality". 30 June 2015, https://littlethings.com

Jarrett, Christian, "What Your Walk Really Says About You". BBC, 19 May 2016, www.bbc.com

Long Live the Sun

Starr, Michelle. "Scientists Have Figured Out When and How Our Sun Will Die". 7 May 2018, www.sciencealert.com

Think Those Pounds Away

Kumar, Aishwarya. "The Grandmaster Diet: How to Lose Weight While Barely Moving". ESPN, 27 April 2020, www.espn.com

Bats – Be a Friend, Not Afraid

"13 Awesome Facts About Bats". U.S. Department of the Interior, 24 October 2017, www.doi.gov

Nunez, Elisa. "Bats, Facts, and Photos". National Geographic, www.nationalgeographic.com

"Bats". Connecticut Department of Energy and Environmental Protection, https://portal.ct.gov

Golf – The Thrill is Gone

Karolinska, Institutet. "Golf Prolongs Life, Swedish Study Finds". 3 June 2008, www.sciencedaily.com

Our Minds – Whose Side are They On?

Cherry, Kendra. "Social Psychology Experiments and Studies". 4 April 2020, www.verywellmind.com

"5 Groundbreaking Social Psychology Experiments". Florida Tech, www.floridatechonline.com

"The 25 Most Influential Psychological Experiments in History". www.onlinepsychologydegree.info

The Butterfly – What's in a Name?

Bouchard, R. Philip. "Word Connections: Butterfly and Ladybug". 30 August 2016, https://medium.com

Mikula, Rick. "Why are They Called Butterflies?". The Butterfly website, https://butterflywebsite.com

Ward, Luke. "30 Beautiful Facts About Butterflies". www.thefactsite.com

Are the Trees Being Silenced?

Grant, Richard. "Do Trees Talk to Each Other?". Smithsonian Magazine, March 2018, www.smithsonianmag.com

Fleming, Nic. "Earth – Plants talk to Each Other Using an Internet of Fungus". BBC, 11 November 2014, www.bbc.com

"Mesopotamia – Tree Spirit Wisdom". https://treespiritwisdom.com

Dolphins vs. Sharks

"How Do Dolphins Communicate? These Facts Will Blow Your Mind". Dolphins Plus, 18 January 2018, https://content.dolphinsplus.com

Rogers, Michael. "50 Amazing Shark Facts". Shark Sider, 9 May 2016, www.sharksider.com

"How Intelligent are Whales and Dolphins?". Whale and Dolphin Conservation, https://us.whales.org

"Amazing Facts about Dolphins". https://onekindplanet.org

"Dolphin Communication". Dolphin Research Center) https://dolphins.org

The Doomsday Dance

Rice, Doyle. "Doomsday Clock Reset to 100 Seconds to Midnight, World's Destruction". USA Today, 23 January 2020, www.usatoday.com

Chow, Denise. "Doomsday Clock Set at 100 Seconds to Midnight – Perilously Close to Catastrophe". NBC News, www.nbcnews.com

"The Doomsday Clock, Explained". University of Chicago News, https://news.uchicago.edu

Made in the USA
Monee, IL
22 July 2022

A TERRIFIED YET OCCASIONALLY OPTIMISTIC
ENVIRONMENTAL SCIENTIST TAKES A HUMOROUS LOOK AT
THE SCIENCE BEHIND THE HUMAN AND ANIMAL BEHAVIORS
THAT MAKE A DOOMED PLANET SO INTERESTING.

If you've ever wanted to get the real dirt on forest bathing without getting muddied, or on animal arsonists without getting burned, or on DIY transcranial Direct Current Stimulation without risking all those excitable neurons that already have one foot out the door, then this is the book for you. Should you be of the type, however, that has found life's little pleasures interrupted of late by the loud ticking of the Doomsday Clock, put in some earplugs, because it's not yet too late to have a good laugh while you learn about 'Cat Research for Dummies,' 'Brain Wars — the Gender Variations,' or 'Boredom — It's Not Just for the Boring.'

In these fifty essays, Bob Lorentson humorously uses science, philosophy, psychology, history, and even poetry to examine a myriad of curious subjects while waiting for the collapse of civilization.

"Cheer up. Things may be getting worse at a slower rate."
Ashleigh Brilliant — *I May Not Be Totally Perfect, But Parts Of Me Are Excellent*